BULLETIN BOARDS PLUS

by
Robyn Freedman Spizman

Illustrated by Vanessa Filkins

Cover by Vanessa Filkins

Copyright © Good Apple, Inc., 1989

ISBN No. 0-86653-510-1

Printing No. 987654321

GOOD APPLE, INC.
BOX 299
CARTHAGE, IL 62321-0299

502744

150 3309

ACKNOWLEDGEMENT

My warmest and deepest thanks go to all the outstanding individuals at Good Apple. It gives me great pride to be a part of the Good Apple family, and I will always be grateful to them for believing in me and helping me bring you the best books possible.

DEDICATION

This book is dedicated to one of the most outstanding and talented educators I've ever known and do sadly miss, Howard Knopf. It was Howard who introduced me to Good Apple and encouraged me to write my first of many books for Good Apple. I will always think of him with much admiration and respect. His unselfish nature and desire for helping others will always be remembered and treasured. Howard, this book's for you.

INTRODUCTION

Bulletin Boards Plus not only brings you an innovative collection of bulletin board ideas, but it will also introduce you to new ideas and territories that await your creative touch. Whether it is on the wall, window or door, a new concept for enhancing your classroom is at your fingertips.

From appealing ceilings to Door Delighters, this book presents a comprehensive theme that can be carried out daily in your classroom. Exciting new ways to deliver a message, reinforce a concept and help you teach a lesson are presented. Children learn by being stimulated in a variety of ways, and *Bulletin Boards Plus* recognizes and encourages that. Each theme in this book is illustrated in a myriad of ways. While the message might change, the theme approach links the moments in a child's day into a captivating world of wonder and enlightenment. Be it dinosaurs or outer space, children enjoy learning when an element of surprise is added. You may wish to create a special award for acknowledging your students' participation. It is my hope that each child will be given one throughout the school year. He/She can earn it by helping create the display or bulletin board and by giving an extra hand in livening up the classroom. Your students are your most valuable resource and will enjoy being involved in the creative process.

Whether you are topping off a table or waking up a window, you and your students' efforts will be noticed and appreciated by all those individuals who pass through your doors daily. I sincerely hope this book brings you the enjoyment that I felt while writing it. Plan, prepare and proudly present!

Best wishes,

Robyn Spizman

GA1080

TABLE OF CONTENTS

GA1080

GA1080

GA1080

HANDS

1

Theme for the Month: HANDS

Use this unit to liven up your classroom while centering your attention around a thumbs-up theme. Enlist all the helping hands at your fingertips and focus your efforts on these handy ideas. Trace them, place them and brighten up your classroom with the following handful of applause-winning displays.

Here's a Door Delighter sure to be inviting to all who enter your classroom. Use this bulletin board to display students' traced handprints cut from construction paper. Each student can bring in a photograph of himself and add it to his hand. These smiling faces are sure to give a warm welcome at your classroom door.

Use this bulletin board to strengthen students' addition and subtraction skills. Instruct students to solve each problem displayed on the hands by filling in the missing numbers. Students can check their work by adding up all the numbers to see if the grand total equals and matches yours.

Use this bulletin board to display student work of any kind that you wish to praise. Reuse this board as often as you wish, but be sure to recognize all students. Even improvement in a particular subject should count. Try recycling the thumbs-up theme by tying a string around each thumb and adding facts or notes that you would like your students to remember.

Create your own Hall of Fame by displaying your students' handprints. Instruct students to write descriptive clues about themselves on their hands, and let classmates guess who's who in your Hands of Fame. For a new twist, add a handprint filled with clues about a famous person in history and challenge your students to identify who it is.

GA1080

Use this bulletin board to encourage students to read books on their reading level. Refer to the hand pattern and use fabric or wallpaper scraps to create the shirt sleeve. Add construction paper baseballs or try pinning foam rubber balls on the board for a special effect. Enhance the board with book jackets or even book reports and encourage high reading averages and home run readers! Students who read five or more books could also earn their names on the board.

All Hands on Deck is the ideal learning center/bulletin board for encouraging your students to practice addition and subtraction. Place two playing cards of matching sets (hearts, clubs) together on the board. Have students add or subtract each and write their answers on paper. Students can change the problems daily by adding new cards or mixing up the current ones. Each day the winning combinations change as your students try their hands at showing off their math skills. Deck the border of this board with cutout hands and leave them blank or use them to write the names of students whose hard work deserves a hand!

Use this bulletin board to involve students in good health habits. Instruct students to write their health tips on index cards. Additional pictures from magazines or labels from nutritious foods can be collected to illustrate the ideas. Add students' ideas until the board is completely filled with points for good health.

Congratulations

to _____

HANDS UP FOR YOU!
We've got to hand it to you for such great work!

GA1080

Use this bulletin board along with index cards to encourage students to focus on manners you wish to see more of. Conduct a brainstorming session and involve students while determining which manners they should reach for. Each student could trace his arm and hand and autograph it every time he displays one of the manners listed.

The previous bulletin board, Reach for Good Manners, could be recycled by writing words on index cards that students can use for a rhyming game. Encourage each student to state how many words he can think of that rhyme with a selected word. Have a class challenge and alternate turns until someone runs out. Whoever is left holding the most words wins the game.

Use this bulletin board to encourage students exploring a variety of shapes to create an overall work of art. Traced hands will ignite their ideas as you challenge each student to transform it into something special. Try putting two together; add paper details or odds and ends for features. Display their creations on the board or try hanging them from coat hangers for a whimsical effect.

Use this bulletin board during November to encourage students to be thankful during the season of Thanksgiving. Use the Hands on Art experience as previously shown to turn hand shapes into turkeys. Ask each student to write what he is thankful for on the body of the turkey and add his feelings to the bulletin board.

4

GA1080

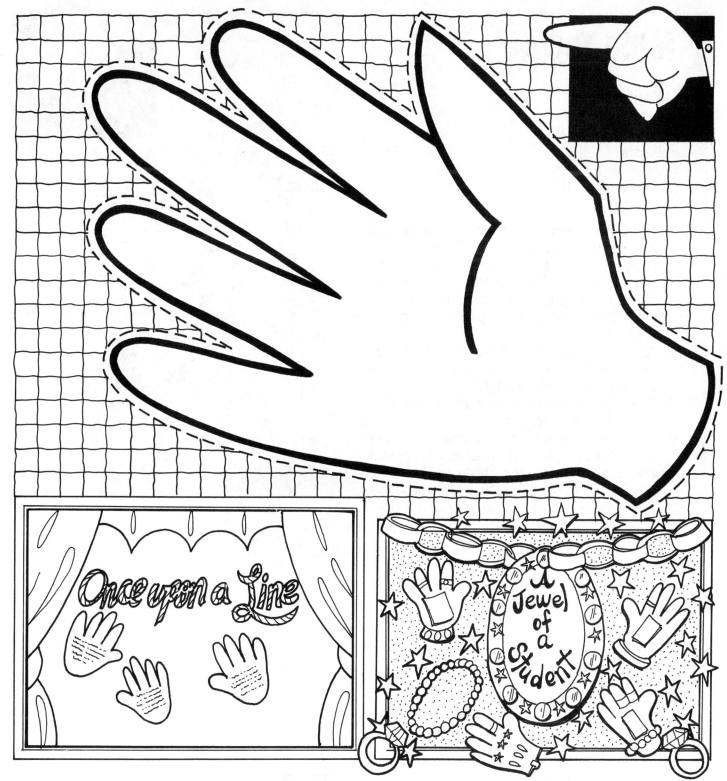

Use this bulletin board to add a new twist to those book reports. Instruct students to trace their hands or duplicate the accompanying pattern and give one to each student. Each student will illustrate the book he reads by drawing characters on the fingers and then writing a short paragraph about the story. A fun game would be to challenge the students to guess the name of each book by viewing its lineup.

Use this bulletin board to put the finishing touch on your hand-filled month. Bedazzle this board by adding rings and bracelets, odds and ends to create a glittering display of your students' cutout hand shapes. Try using bottle tops, paper chains, aluminum foil and a sparkling assortment of throwaways. This board is a surefire way to recycle all those hands and transform trash into treasures.

5

Table Topper

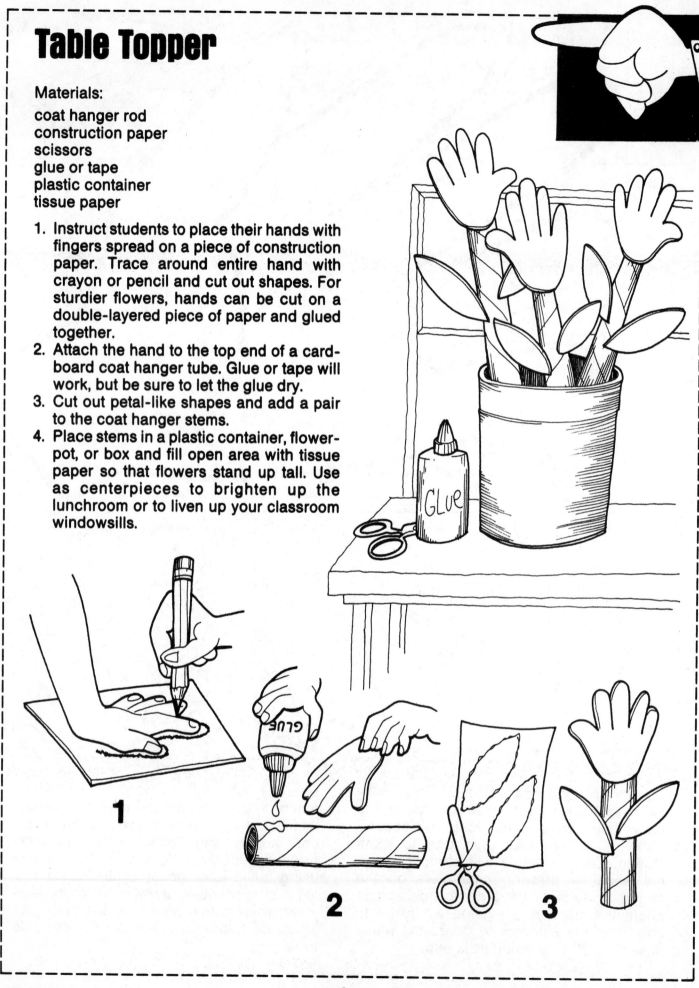

Materials:

coat hanger rod
construction paper
scissors
glue or tape
plastic container
tissue paper

1. Instruct students to place their hands with fingers spread on a piece of construction paper. Trace around entire hand with crayon or pencil and cut out shapes. For sturdier flowers, hands can be cut on a double-layered piece of paper and glued together.
2. Attach the hand to the top end of a cardboard coat hanger tube. Glue or tape will work, but be sure to let the glue dry.
3. Cut out petal-like shapes and add a pair to the coat hanger stems.
4. Place stems in a plastic container, flowerpot, or box and fill open area with tissue paper so that flowers stand up tall. Use as centerpieces to brighten up the lunchroom or to liven up your classroom windowsills.

Glue

1

2

3

GA1080

Window Wake-Up

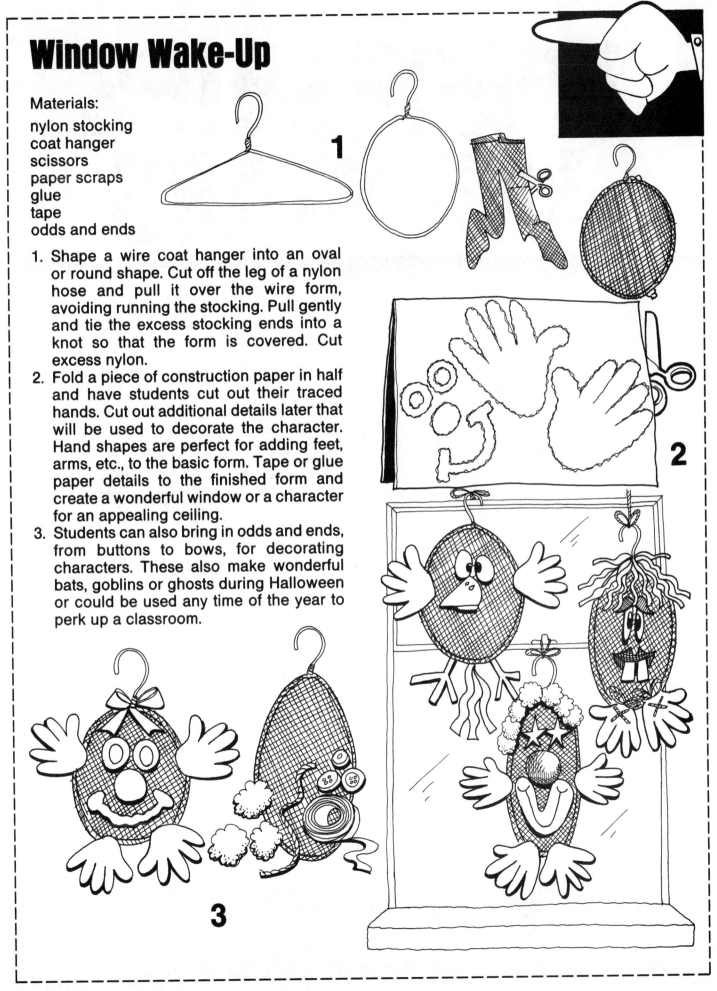

Materials:

nylon stocking
coat hanger
scissors
paper scraps
glue
tape
odds and ends

1. Shape a wire coat hanger into an oval or round shape. Cut off the leg of a nylon hose and pull it over the wire form, avoiding running the stocking. Pull gently and tie the excess stocking ends into a knot so that the form is covered. Cut excess nylon.
2. Fold a piece of construction paper in half and have students cut out their traced hands. Cut out additional details later that will be used to decorate the character. Hand shapes are perfect for adding feet, arms, etc., to the basic form. Tape or glue paper details to the finished form and create a wonderful window or a character for an appealing ceiling.
3. Students can also bring in odds and ends, from buttons to bows, for decorating characters. These also make wonderful bats, goblins or ghosts during Halloween or could be used any time of the year to perk up a classroom.

GA1080

SPACESHIPS AND STARS

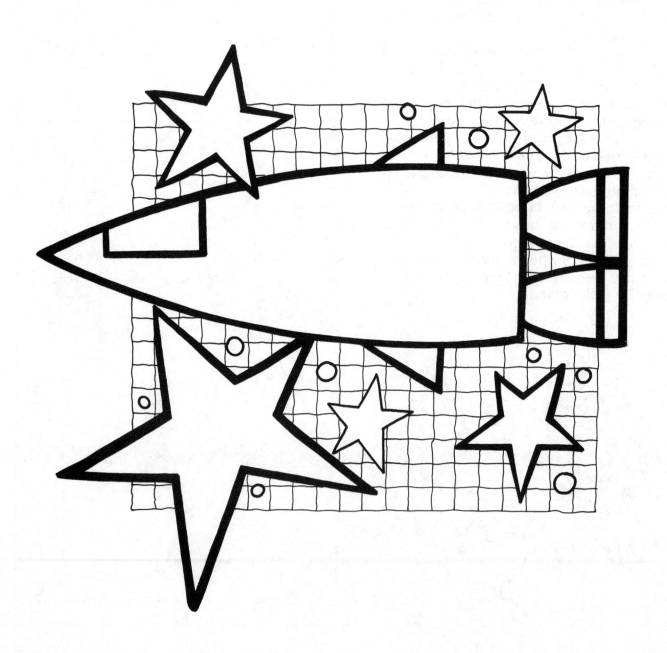

8

Theme for the Month: SPACESHIPS AND STARS

Soar your students along with the following ideas sure to ignite their imaginations and challenge their minds. This unit lends itself to a perfect takeoff whether it's at the beginning of the school year, the first of a new calendar year or the countdown as the year comes to an end. Your students will jump aboard as you fly into a month-long journey filled with fun and facts.

Door Delighter: Your students will take the starring role as you display their names on your star-studded classroom door. Begin by covering the door with blue bulletin board display paper. Precut one star for each student and add his name. Students could do the writing and outline each letter with glue. Glitter could be sprinkled over the star for a sparkling effect. Try this while working over a shoe box, and shake the excess glitter off the star to be sure that it is applied properly. Add tissue paper streamers to each star for a three-dimensional flair. Save the stars and reuse them at students' desks to identify them during PTA night or as an alternate Door Delighter entitled "Starring Mrs. _____'s Class."

Use the name tag pattern and duplicate rockets to cover the bulletin board. Add tissue paper streamers to the base of the rocket by gluing or stapling them in place and create a soaring three-dimensional effect. On each rocket, write a sequence of numbers leaving out some of the answers. Send students on a mission to find the missing numbers and fill in the answers on their own page. Rockets can be alternated or the opposite side used to add new problems for your students to encounter.

GA1080

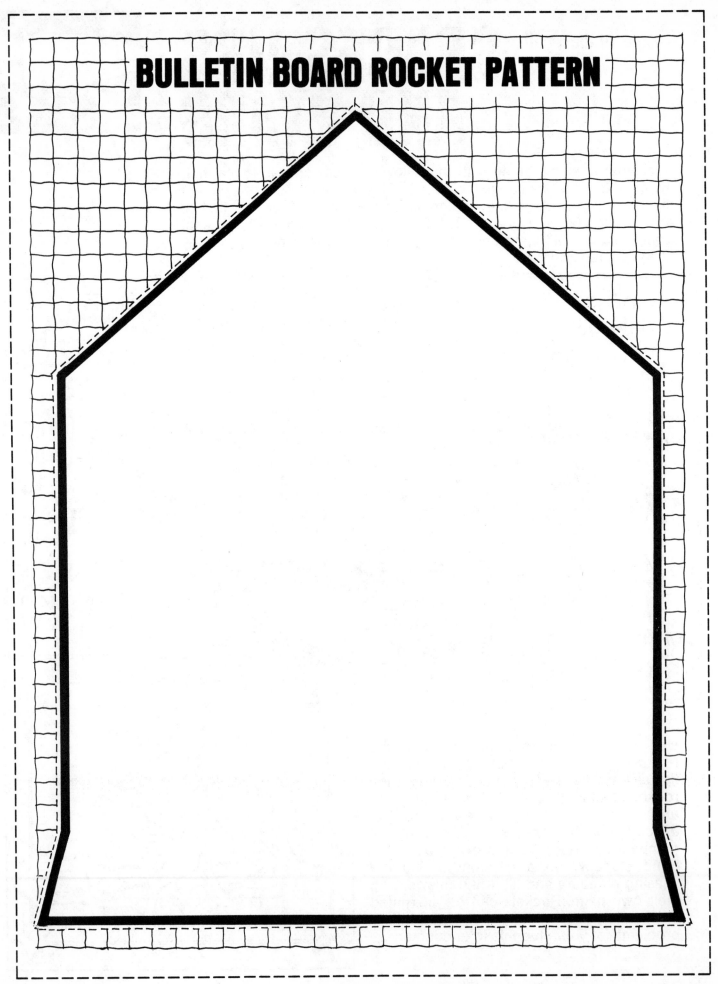

BULLETIN BOARD ROCKET PATTERN

GA1080

NAME TAG PATTERN

_____

NAME

Use this bulletin board to build math skills. Instruct students to subtract the rocket number each day from the numbers on the stars. Your rocket can be changed daily for a new assignment, or students could use this as a game that the entire class could play. Divide the class into two teams and give each side a try. Points are awarded for correct answers, and a running tally could be kept for rematches.

Use this bulletin board to challenge students to use their spelling skills by making letter combinations to spell words. Pin the letters of the alphabet along the border of this bulletin board. Use it as a learning center and have students take turns at combining any of the letters to make as many words as possible. Each student could keep a dictionary list of his winning words and new words can be added daily.

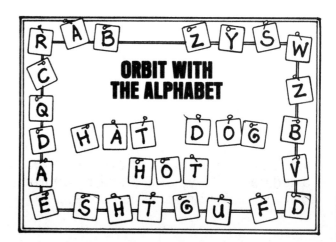

11

GA1080

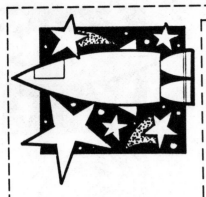

Home will be your students' destination with this special award as you send Rocket Grams to brag about good work, good deeds or improvement in students' skills.

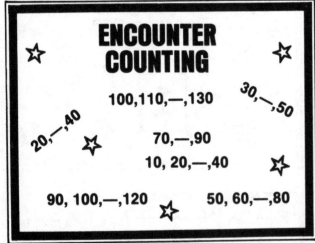

ROCKET GRAM

To: _____

Student of the Week

From: _____

_____

_____
Signed

ENCOUNTER COUNTING

100,110,—,130   30,—,50

20,—,40

70,—,90

10, 20,—,40

90, 100,—,120   50, 60,—,80

WE'RE SPELLING ALL-STARS

graph   solar   laugh   green   planet   rotate

Kim, Ann, Justin, Bob, Gary

Use this bulletin board to reinforce your students' ability to identify numbers by name and put them in order. This display could also be used to encourage counting by ones, fives, tens, etc. In any sequence leave out a number and have students fill in the missing blank to make the sequence correct.

Use this bulletin board to motivate students to learn spelling words. Try having a classwide spelling bee and add the winners' names each day to brighten up the moon. Display spelling words on the stars and rotate them weekly. Add additional words for students to learn, look up in the dictionary and use in stories for a fun creative writing exercise.

GA1080

AIM
FOR GOOD MANNERS

Use this display to encourage students to focus on good manners. Have a brainstorming session and write students' ideas on the rocket ships. When a student displays one of the good manners, have him add his name to the planet.

Use this bulletin board to display student work that is soaring with neatness. Encourage good penmanship and let students choose the work that they are proudest of. Selections can be changed weekly and can focus on different strengths which you wish to enhance.

Use this bulletin board to promote students' reading books about faraway places. Add suggestions to the board by displaying book jackets which are possible choices. These could include books about other countries or cultures, outer space or anything that is far from us in distance.

13

Appealing Ceilings

Here are two activities which students will enjoy. These mobiles will hang from the ceiling, once suspended from a string, and will brighten up your classroom.

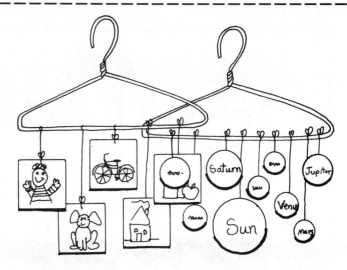

Moon Beam Mobile: Instruct students to decide what they would take if they were going to live on the moon. Students can illustrate their objects or cut out pictures from magazines and glue them to construction paper. Suspend pictures from string tied to a coat hanger and adjust them accordingly to make sure that they balance. This lesson offers the perfect opportunity to discuss balance since the mobile will not hang properly if the weight is not equally distributed.

Solar Mobile: Use this project as an optional mobile as you study planets. Each student can make his own solar system and use paper cutouts, string and a coat hanger to make a model perfect for displaying.

Duplicate this award and have it at your fingertips to use for praising your students for improvement in a subject.

Student's Name

Orbiting with Good Work

14

GA1080

FRUITS AND VEGETABLES

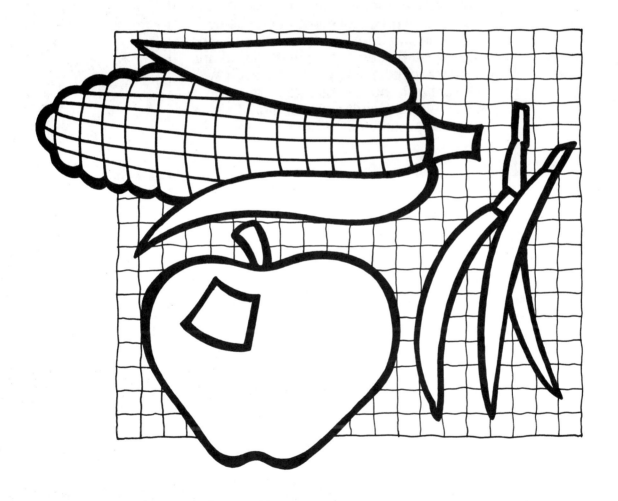

15

Theme for the Month: FRUITS AND VEGETABLES

WE RELISH THESE STUDENTS

Use this Door Delighter to let students know they are the pick of the crop! Students can create paper vegetables and display their photographs on them or cut out magazine illustrations and collage the paper-covered door. This is a perfect welcome to your classroom and a way to focus positive attention on each and every classmate.

Use this Door Delighter to welcome students to your classroom. Shades of green tissue paper or even green toilet paper can be used to create textured lettuce to be added to the board. Small pieces can be wadded up and glued to a circular shape. Wrap each with clear cellophane or plastic wrap for a realistic effect. Heads will certainly turn as your class proudly displays their pick of the crop.

"LETTUCE" WELCOME YOU TO OUR CLASS

Use this bulletin board to ignite your students' imaginations for a creative writing lesson. Reuse fruits and vegetables or make new ones from the patterns and display them on the board. Write a story starter on each and challenge each student to ripen the idea by turning it into a story.

16

GA1080

Use this bulletin board to display students' work that is appealing. Begin by having each student bring in a banana. Have an edible art lesson and instruct students to draw the banana in its original form. Then let them peel it a little and draw it again. Next have students take a bite and continue to draw it until only the peel is left. Students can color and then cut out their favorite drawings which can be added to the board for a finishing touch.

Instruct students to plant their thoughts and feelings on this board. Promote good will and thinking of others by encouraging each student to add something nice or special about someone else.

Use this bulletin board to welcome students to your classroom. Cut out one round shape per student and add his name. Put all the shapes together to form the bunch of grapes and top it off with a triangular stem. You could involve your students by having them curve the corners of a square shape and learn how to create a round one. Your bunch is sure to eat up this board and love seeing their names as part of the bunch.

Use this bulletin board to cart and display all of your students' work which you are proud of. This board is perfect for any subject and a student of the week can reload it from week to week.

GA1080

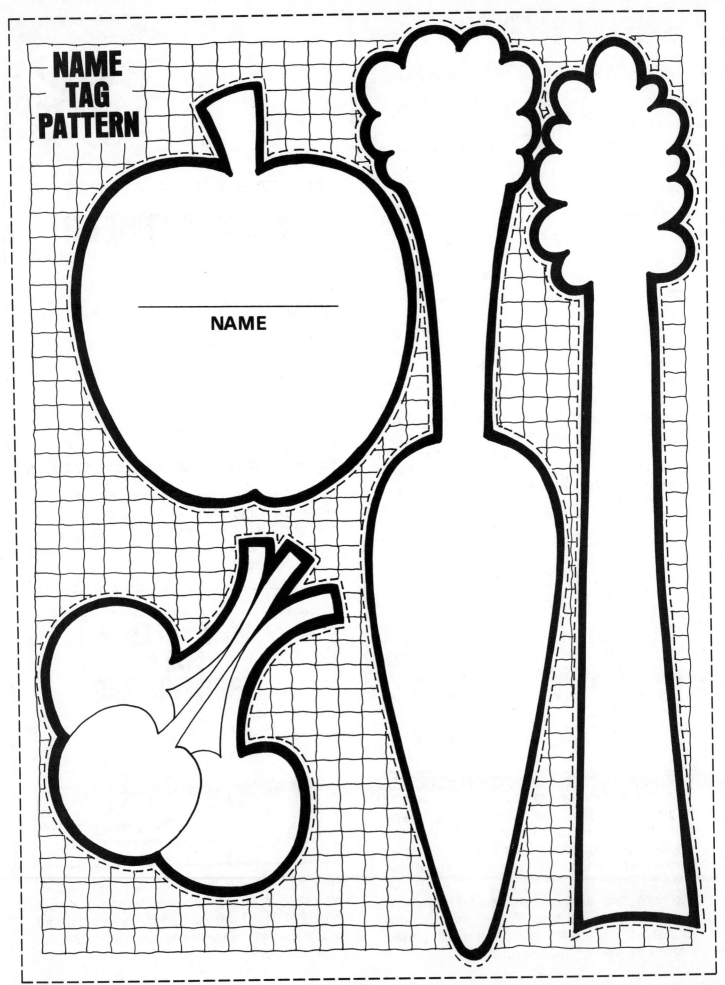

NAME
TAG
PATTERN

_____
NAME

18

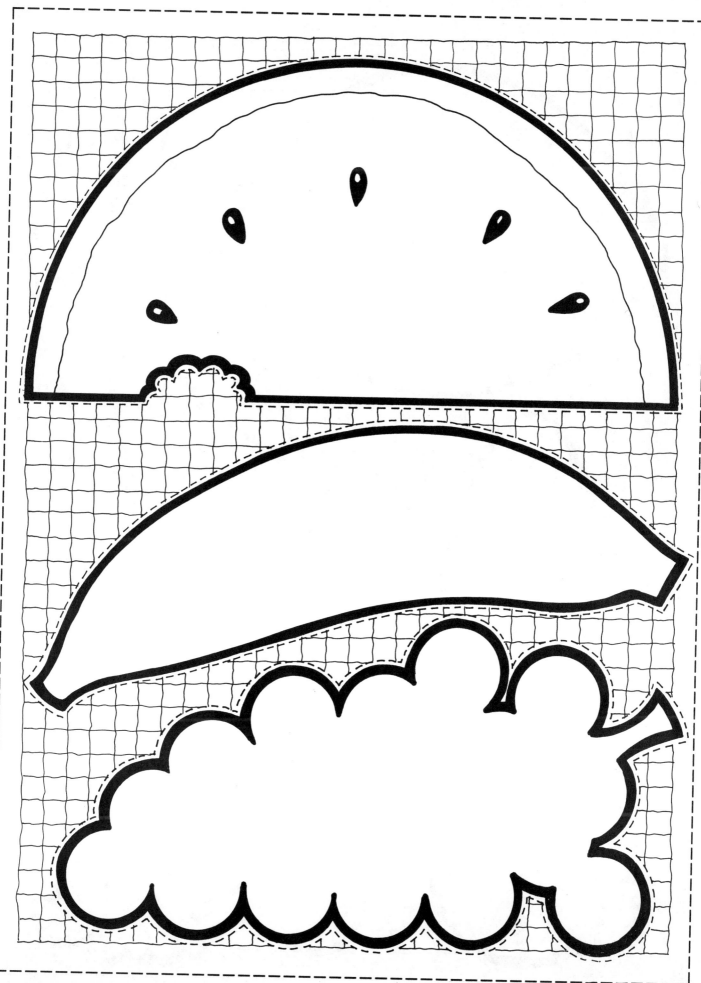

19

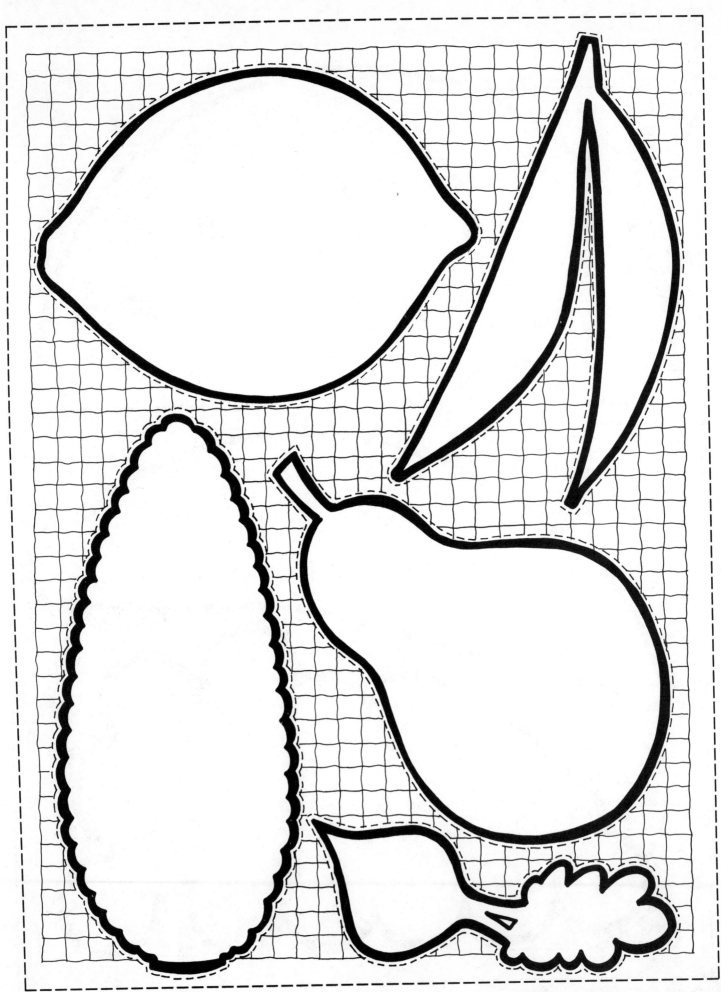

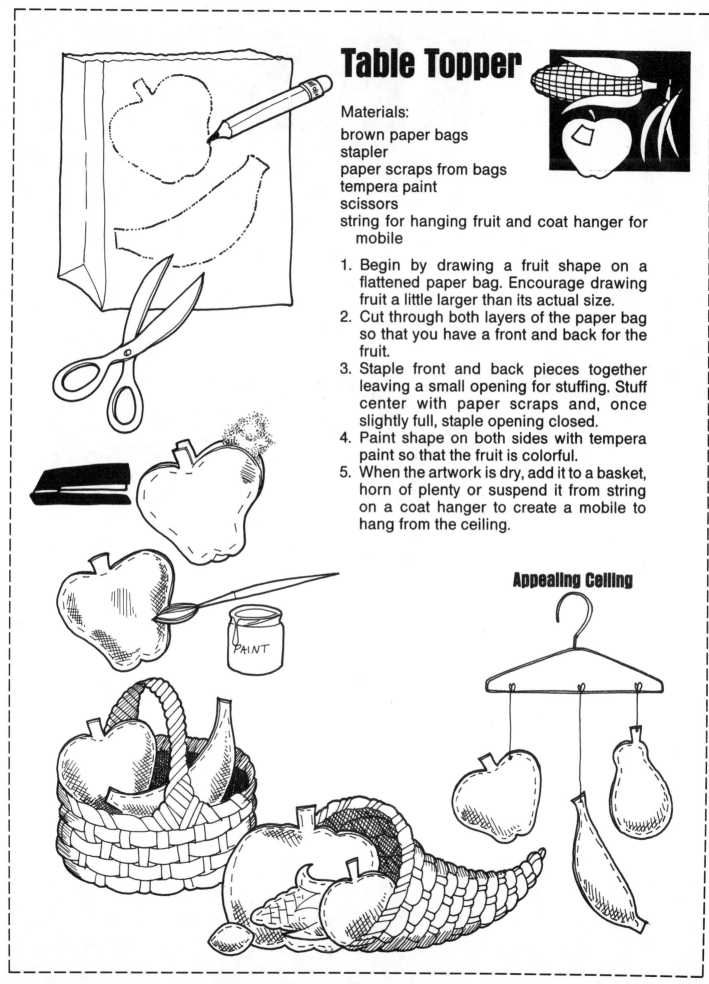

Table Topper

Materials:

brown paper bags
stapler
paper scraps from bags
tempera paint
scissors
string for hanging fruit and coat hanger for
mobile

1. Begin by drawing a fruit shape on a flattened paper bag. Encourage drawing fruit a little larger than its actual size.
2. Cut through both layers of the paper bag so that you have a front and back for the fruit.
3. Staple front and back pieces together leaving a small opening for stuffing. Stuff center with paper scraps and, once slightly full, staple opening closed.
4. Paint shape on both sides with tempera paint so that the fruit is colorful.
5. When the artwork is dry, add it to a basket, horn of plenty or suspend it from string on a coat hanger to create a mobile to hang from the ceiling.

Appealing Ceiling

PAINT

21

KEYS

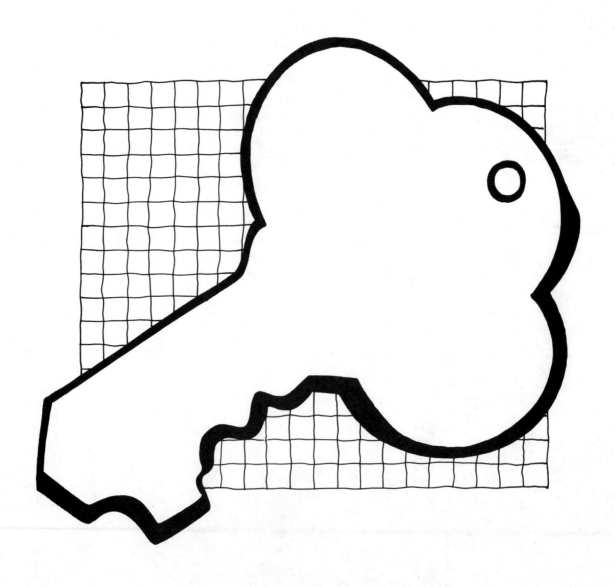

GA1080

Theme for the Month: # KEYS

Use this bulletin board to suggest opening lines for starting a story. Duplicate the key pattern and write a story starter on each. Encourage students to select one and develop it into a story.

Use this Door Delighter to introduce your students. Duplicate a key pattern for each student and add his name. Mix up the keys and give them out to students and set the timer for five minutes. Whoever finds his key and returns the one he has to the correct person wins. Keys can then be added to the door for a perfect opener to your room.

Use this bulletin board to display words you want your students to key in on. Key words could also include spelling lessons, new vocabulary words or words to look up in the dictionary.

GA1080

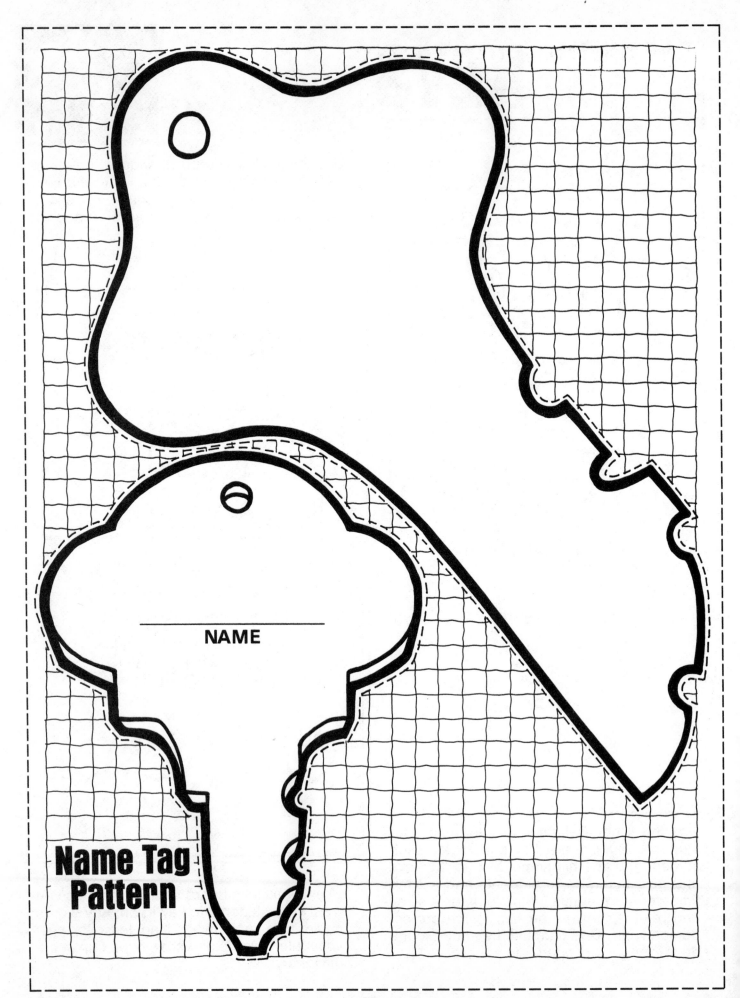

NAME

Name Tag Pattern

24

GA1080

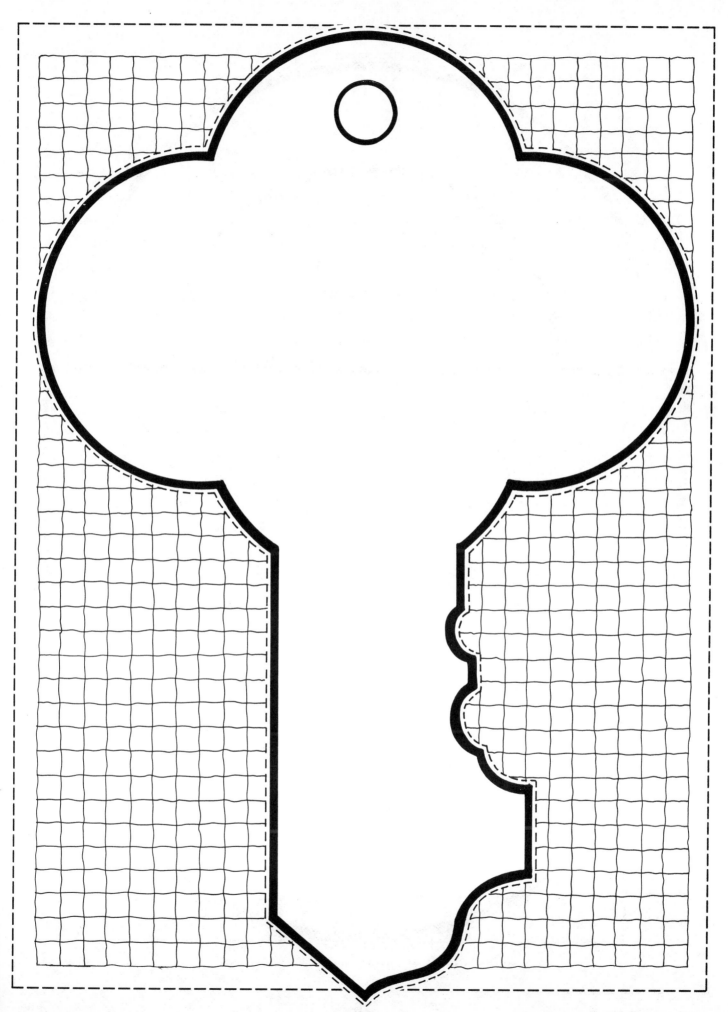

25

GA1080

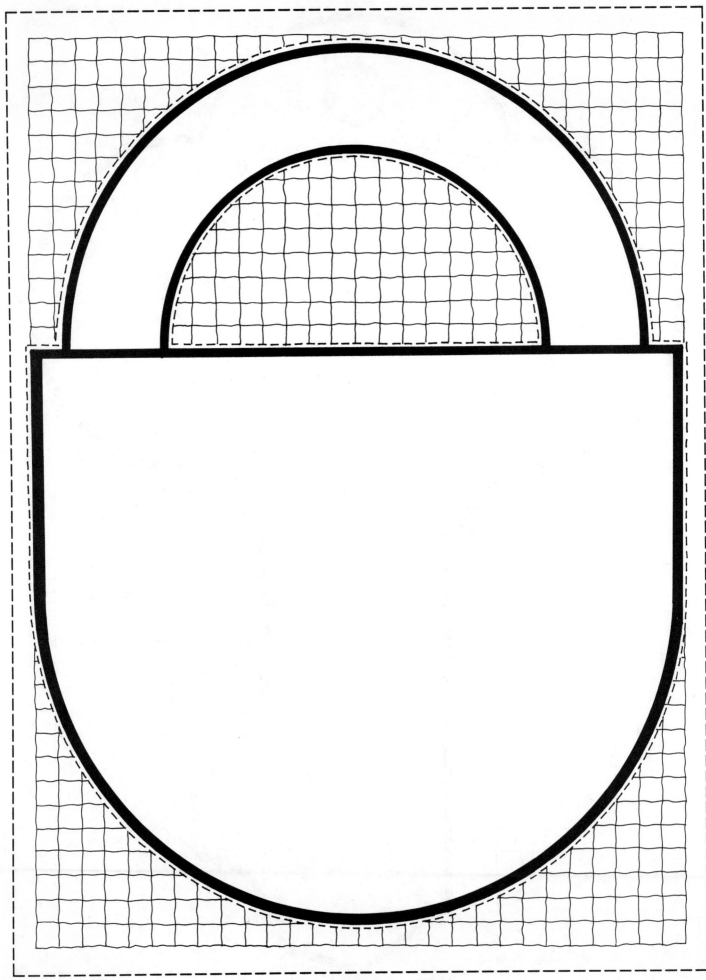

26

GA1080

WE ARE KEYED UP FOR SPELLING

Use this learning center to reinforce visual discrimination. In one box place keys with the letters of a word mixed up and in the other box place the actual word spelled properly. Challenge students to select a mixed up word and key in on its correct match from the opposite box.

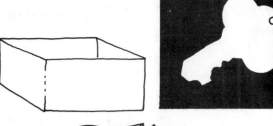

WORD CARD PATTERN

UNLOCK THE MYSTERIES OF SCIENCE

Use this bulletin board to encourage students to think about specific scientific discoveries. From gravity to the wheel, encourage students to bring in illustrations to be added to the board that are based on principles that you are studying in science.

KEYS TO OUR FUTURE

Medicine ° Agriculture ° Transportation
° Food Service ° Mechanic
° Jeweler ° Writer ° Teacher

Use this bulletin board to focus your students' attention on careers. Add a variety of careers to the keys on the board and assign one to each student to investigate and write a report on. Students could interview someone of that profession or read about it. Add reports to the bulletin board by each appropriate key.

GA1080

Use this bulletin board to promote an awareness of physical fitness. Duplicate a key pattern for each student and write his name on it. Add the keys to the board, and as each student completes or does a specific task which contributes to his fitness (takes a walk, exercises, etc.), let him add a star or sticker by his name.

Use this bulletin board to challenge students to find the missing answer. Display a math problem on each key and alternate them weekly with new ones. Instruct students to unlock each and find the right answer.

Here's the perfect bulletin board for displaying facts you want your students to remember. Duplicate the keys or reuse ones previously created and add facts or things to remember on each. As students master them, they can autograph the bulletin board with their own names.

28

GA1080

MUSICAL/ PIANO

29

Theme for the Month:

MUSICAL/PIANO

Use this unit to liven up your classroom with an entire combo of ideas that are sure to bring music to your students' ears. Encourage students who actually play musical instruments to join in and show off their talents as you sing your way through a month filled with the sounds of learning.

Here's a Door Delighter sure to tune every-one in on your classroom's theme. Trace a musical note for each student from the basic pattern and place each student's name on one. Add all of the notes to the covered door and sound off a big welcome to your students.

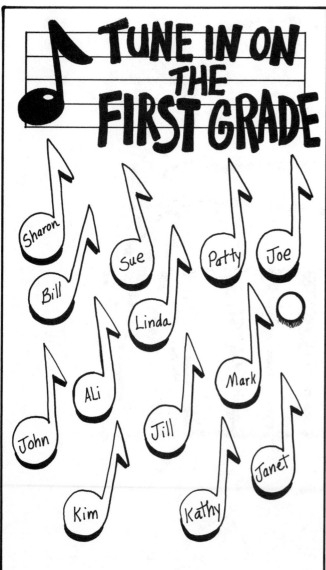

Use this bulletin board to show off the outstanding performances of your students' work. Reuse this board as often as you wish to motivate students to improve handwriting skills, focus on neatness or sharpen up their skills in math.

GA1080

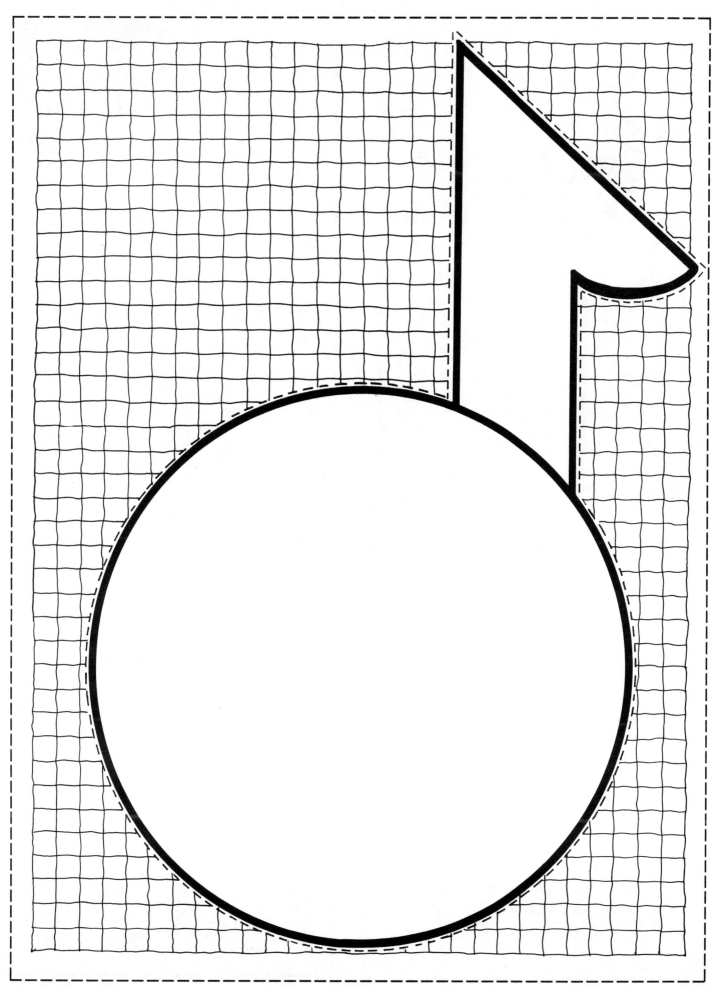

31

GA1080

Use this bulletin board to display reports that relate to science. From famous scientists to exciting scientific discoveries, this bulletin board can show off your students' work. Substitute any subject here and this bulletin board can be recycled and used over and over again. Example: SOUND OFF IN SOCIAL STUDIES or SOUND OFF IN READING.

Here's an easy to make bulletin board perfect for displaying the alphabet. Write each alphabet letter on a muscial note and then place them on the board randomly. Students can try their turn at putting the notes in order to show they are all tuned up.

Use this bulletin board to highlight a variety of current events. Encourage students to be in charge of cutting them out of the newspaper and updating them regularly.

Trace the musical notes from the pattern and post them by facts or suggestions you want your students to notice. From current events to classroom rules, use this board as a message center or a reinforcer for any subject you desire.

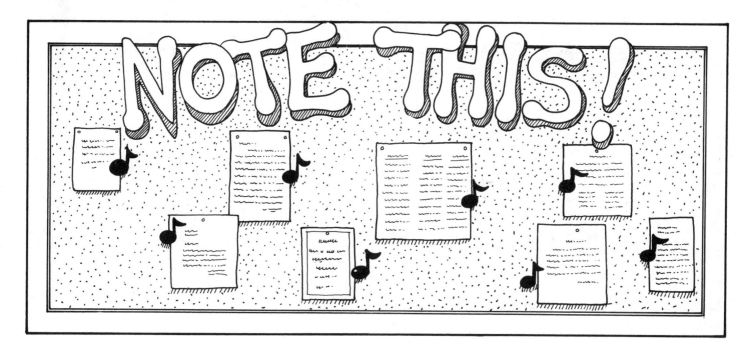

Reuse the musical note from the previous bulletin board and create a perfect display for any holiday season. Students can use this bulletin board and create a graffiti mural filled with notes to wish other students in the class good cheer. From Thanksgiving to Christmas to Hanukkah, this board could be purposely used as a place students can exhibit their thoughtfulness while thinking of others.

33

Here's the ideal bulletin board for displaying thank-you notes written by students. Add the musical notes by each student's work with his name by his note. Notes of thanks could be written to community helpers, school workers or anyone who deserves to be noted for his/her hard work.

Use this bulletin board as a learning center to strengthen students' addition, subtraction, multiplication or division skills. On each key of the piano on this bulletin board, write a math combination. Staple the key so that it can be lifted up and write the answer underneath. Students can try their turn at playing the keys and checking their answers right on the spot.

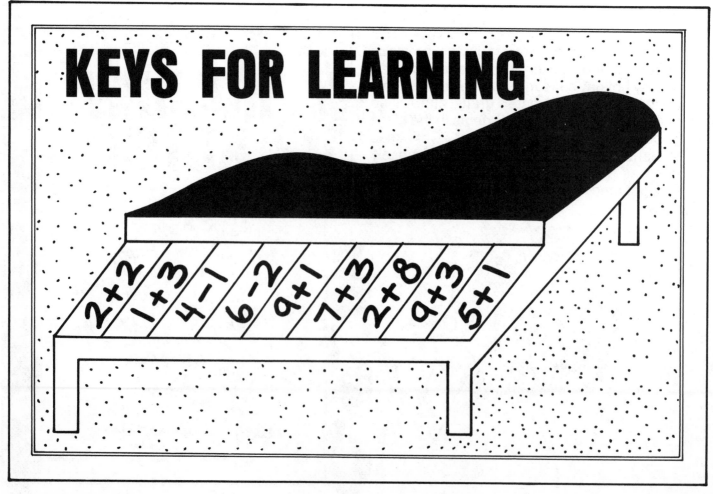

GA1080

MUSIC TO OUR EARS

PIANO

Use this bulletin board to teach students about the variety of musical instruments and their correct names. Have students search for magazine pictures and bring them in to add to the bulletin board. Label each on an index card and place them in an envelope that is stapled to the board. Students can try their matching skills by placing the cards on the board by their mates. The student who follows could check the previous student's work and then mix up the cards and try his hand at it.

Student's Name

IS TUNED UP IN

Subject

GA1080

DINOSAURS

36

Theme for the Month: DINOSAURS

Your students will love this month's theme as you invade your room with prehistoric creatures. From a triceratop to a stegosaurus, your students will be thrilled to explore learning along with these fascinating reptiles.

Here's a Door Delighter sure to welcome your students with a theme they'll all love. Trace the basic dinosaur pattern and add a student's name to each.

PRESCHOOL PREVIEW

THIS CLASS ADORES DINOSAURS

JOE · Lori · Dustin · LISA · Max · Peter · Ava · TINA

Use this bulletin board as a learning center for introducing prefixes. Trace the dinosaur pattern and choose a prefix for the day. Brainstorm with your students all the words they can think of and add each on an index card to a dinosaur. Preview a new word daily and encourage students to keep a record.

GA1080

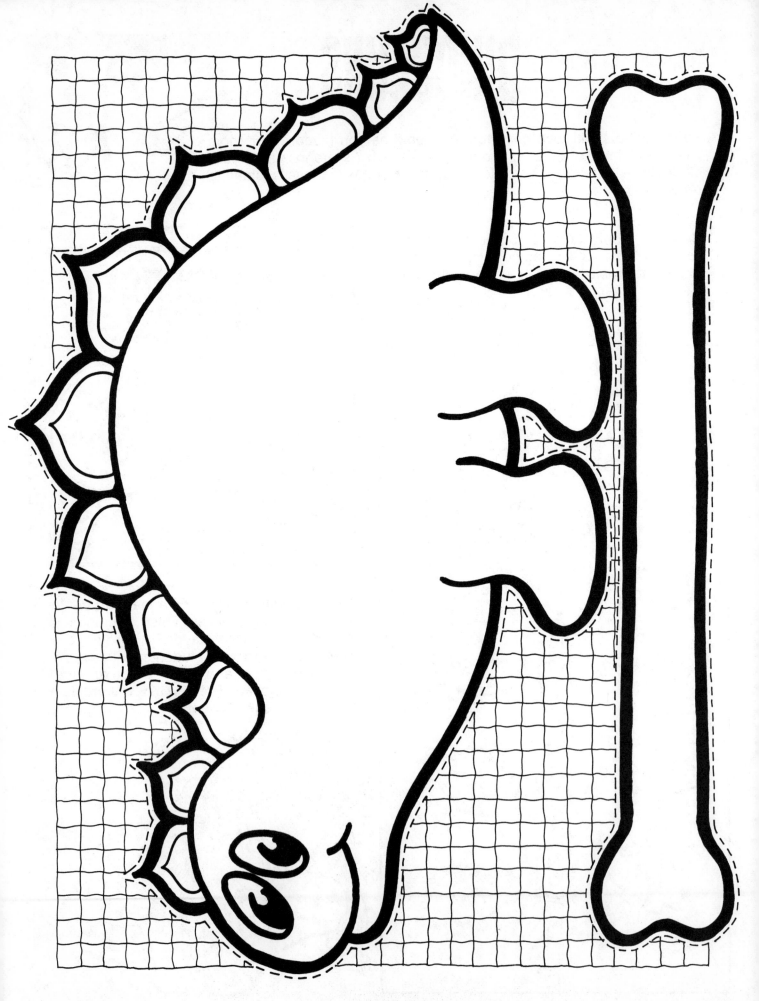

38

GA1080

Use this bulletin board as the perfect place to show off students' prehistoric creations. From books on dinosaurs to illustrations and posters, fill your room with a variety of creatures. Use construction paper, scissors and glue and let your students create their own. Add their names to their work and brighten up your door with these adorable but beasty friends.

Here's the perfect bulletin board for assigning classroom chores to students. Reuse students' dinosaurs with their names on them and assign jobs by placing theirs by particular chores.

Use this bulletin board as an activity center to increase your students' ability to visually discriminate and match patterns. From wallpaper books or patterned fabrics, cut a pair of dinosaurs using the dinosaur pattern. Staple one shape from each pair to the board and place its mate in an envelope pinned at the bottom. Students can try their hand at matching and then pin them in place.

39

GA1080

Use this bulletin board to play an alphabet game. Write each alphabet letter on a dinosaur duplicated from the pattern. Place the dinosaurs in an envelope attached to the board. Cut out one picture of an object or thing that begins with each letter and staple them to the board. Let students have their try at placing all the dinosaurs next to the pictures that begin with the letters.

Table Topper

Materials:

paper plates—small white ones
green tempera paint or markers
scissors
construction paper—assorted colors
glue

1. Give each student a paper plate and construction paper and encourage him to cut out shapes to add to the paper plate body to create a dinosaur.
2. Paint paper plate green (if desired) and let dry. Magic markers could also be used in a variety of colors.
3. Have students glue features to the plates to create their finished products.
4. Attach dinosaurs to cans covered in construction paper and use to top off the tables in your classroom or students' desks.

40

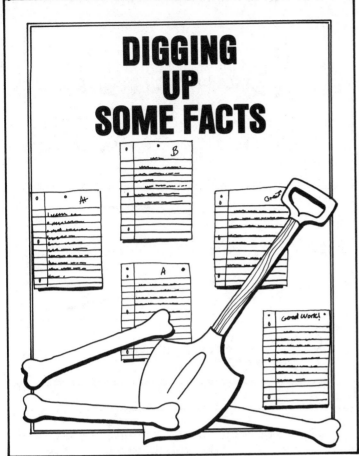

DIGGING UP SOME FACTS

Use this bulletin board to send your students on a search for facts about things that happened long ago. Students could investigate any topic from dinosaurs to fossils. Have each student write a report about his findings and add to the bulletin board.

Use this bulletin board to encourage students to be aware of good manners. Post specifics that you want to encourage and each time a student exhibits one, let him autograph the dinosaur on the board for positive recognition.

41

GA1080

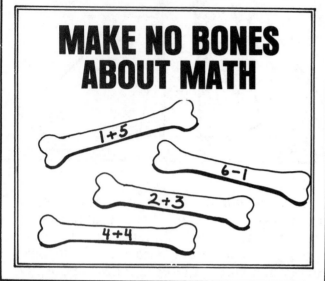

MAKE NO BONES ABOUT MATH

1+5

6-1

2+3

4+4

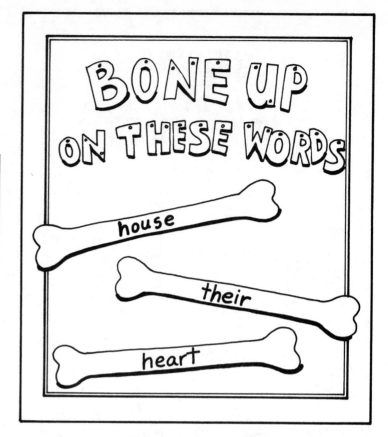

BONE UP ON THESE WORDS

house

their

heart

Here's a learning center perfect for enhancing students' math skills. On each bone write a math problem and change the problems daily. Instruct students to solve the problems and record their answers.

Use this bulletin board to motivate students to bone up on their spelling skills. List your spelling words for the day or week. Add new words to the opposite side of the bones used on the board for math and have students look them up in the dictionary and master their spellings.

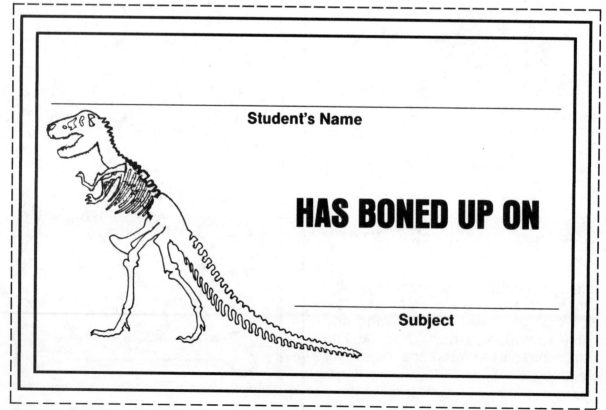

Student's Name

HAS BONED UP ON

Subject

GA1080

FOOTPRINTS

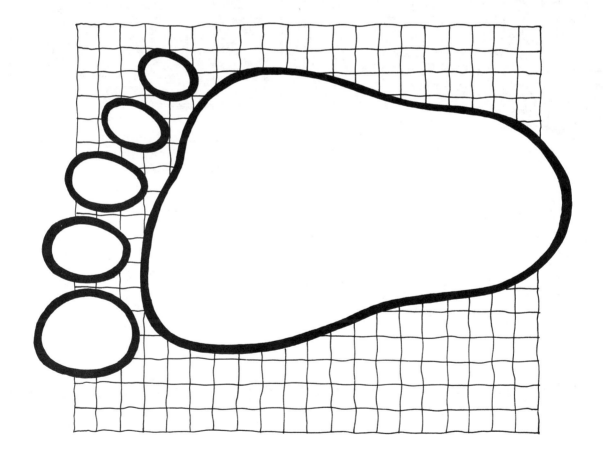

43

Theme for the Month: FOOTPRINTS

Step right up for a month filled with a theme that will knock your students' socks off! From head to toe, your students will surely get a kick out of these ideas.

Here's a Door Delighter sure to welcome anyone who steps up to your classroom door. Instruct each student to trace his foot on a piece of paper and cut it out. Add students' names to their footprints and use them to cover the door.

Here's the perfect bulletin board to show off the strides your students are making in any subject. From neat work to following instructions, your students will feel great about putting their best foot forward!

Use this bulletin board to encourage students' awareness of physical fitness. Surround the bulletin board border with footprints. Add illustrations or cutouts of a variety of activities which contribute to physical fitness. When a student gets a kick out of one of these, he can add his name to a footprint.

44

GA1080

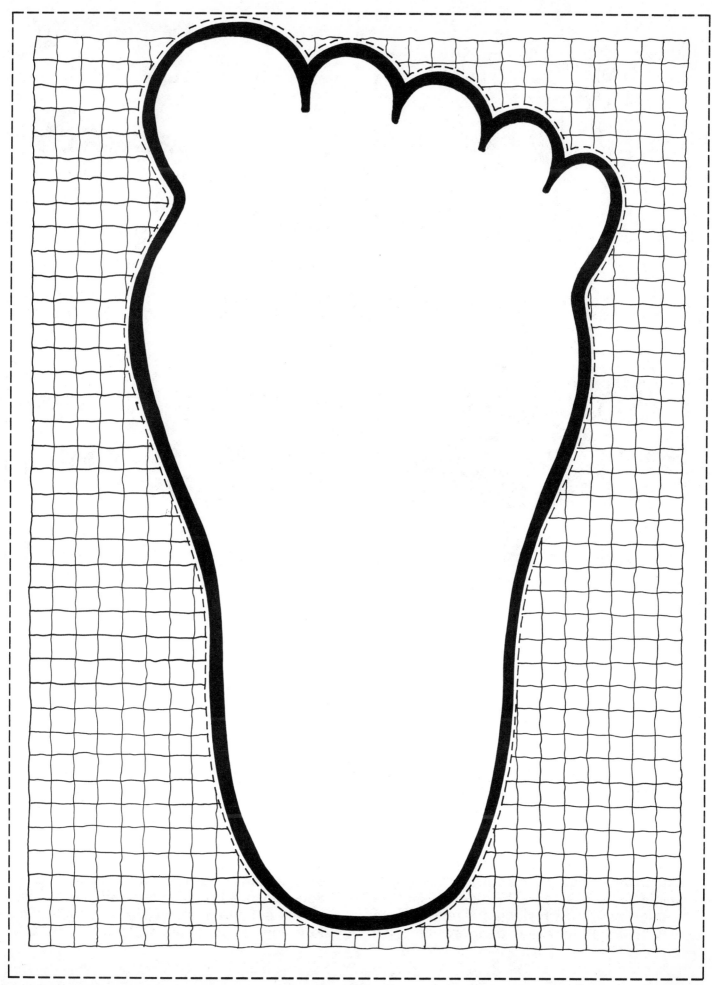

45

Use this bulletin board to build students' math skills. Add addition, subtraction, multiplication or division problems on the footprints on the board. Instruct students to walk their way through each one, answering the math problems on a numbered sheet of paper. Students could check themselves with a master key you make up daily and keep a record of how many they answered correctly.

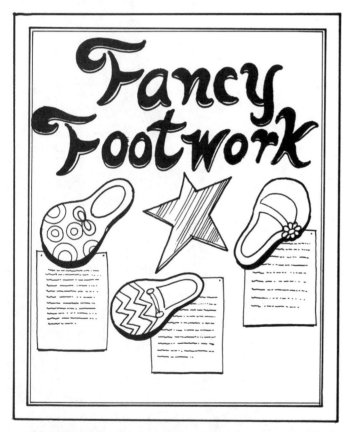

Here's a fun art activity to get your students involved in a colorful project. Each student can trace his own foot and then turn it into a shoe. From polka-dotted sneakers with yarn laces to star-studded shoes ready for a celebration, each shoe can be transformed into a work of art. A new twist for this board might be to assign each student a famous person and have him write a report about what it would be like to be in that person's shoes.

Use this bulletin board to encourage a creative writing lesson. Each student should write a story about the foot stomping things he plans to do this summer. Let him illustrate it and add his story and artwork to the bulletin board. Foot stomping activities could be jumping off the diving board, hiking up a mountain or playing soccer. Whatever the activity, encourage ideas which students can do in their spare time and look forward to.

46

GA1080

Here's a perfect bulletin board to highlight facts your students have learned in a particular subject. Cut out a footprint for each student and add it with his name to the bulletin board. Each time he masters a fact, have him add it to his footprint. This bulletin board will be useful when studying multiplication, science or spelling.

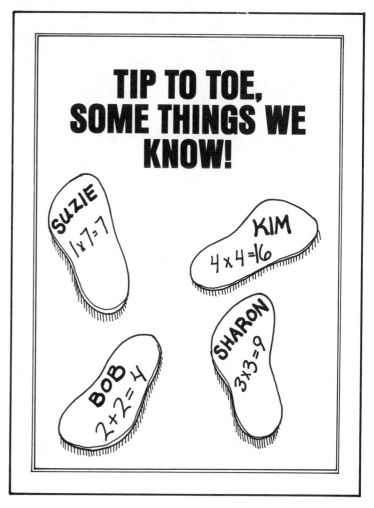

TIP TO TOE, SOME THINGS WE KNOW!

SUZIE
1 x 7 = 7

KIM
4 x 4 = 16

BOB
2 + 2 = 4

SHARON
3 x 3 = 9

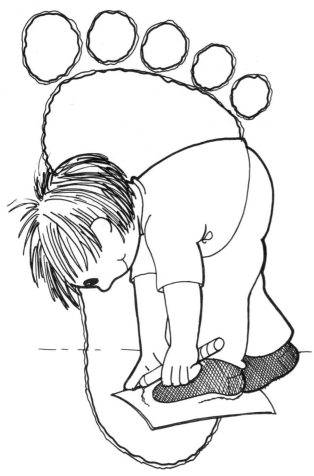

Encourage each student to get a jump on good nutrition by bringing in labels from cans, packages, etc., and adding them to the bulletin board. One side of the bulletin board could be items that keep us hopping and feeling good, and the other side could be foods that contribute to our stopping.

GET A JUMP ON GOOD NUTRITION

HOPPING   STOPPING

47

GA1080

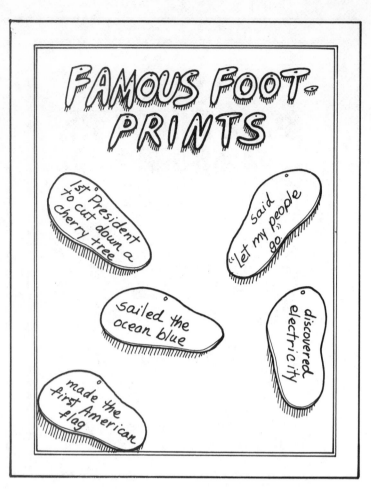

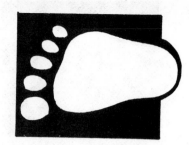

Here's a creative writing exercise perfect for your students. Duplicate a footprint for each student and let him write on it descriptions of a famous person Add all the footprints to the board and let students try to guess who is who.

Here's the perfect bulletin board for encouraging your students to read more books. Duplicate a footprint for each student and have him add his name. Place all the footprints on the left side of the bulletin board and number the top half of the board. As each student reads a book, he gets to step right up to the next number. When a student reaches your class goal, let him earn extra library time or free time coupons for special activities.

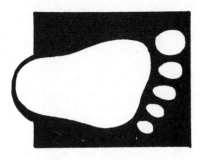

Use this bulletin board to display facts of any kind that you want your students to learn.

Window Wake-Up

Materials:

construction paper
scissors
tape

1. Have students trace around their shoes on construction paper. Trace both right and left feet.
2. Tape feet on windows for a colorful addition to your footprint scheme.

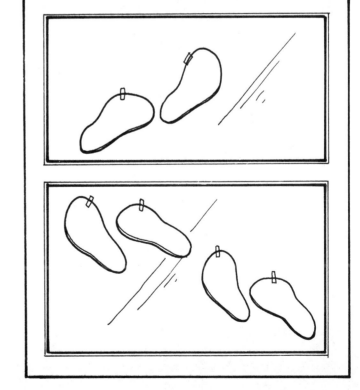

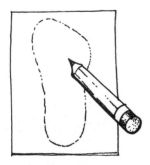

GA1080

CARS

50

Theme for the Month: CARS

Add some get-up-and-go with this automotive unit. Students will love traveling along with this unit on wheels while enjoying every mile of it.

Use this Door Delighter to announce your classroom cargo. Each student can decorate his car according to his preference and add his name. Display your cargo on the classroom door for all to view.

Use this bulletin board to encourage students' awareness of what they can be thankful for. Ignite a classroom discussion on what you have that is precious to you. Trace a car for each student and add his ideas to it. Their precious cargo can be displayed on the bulletin board.

Mrs. Leed's Cargo

Sara
Rob
David
Lou
Jenny
Meg
Phillip
Alice

PRECIOUS CARGO

mom Dad Julie
trees
food
gold jewels silver
pet friends health

Terry

51

Use this bulletin board to encourage students to read books on their reading level. Refer to the car pattern and duplicate one for each student. Have students add their names to the cars and put them on the bulletin board. Each time the student reads a new book, instruct him to add its title to his car.

Use this bulletin board to encourage students to read more books. Refer to the car pattern and after each student reads a specific number of books, add a star to his car for his efforts. Let him then be the "Car Star" for buckling up with a specific number of books.

Use this bulletin board to assign science activities for students to do. From looking for four-leaf clovers to studying an insect for five minutes, add new ideas weekly to the cars for igniting your students' curiosity.

52

GA1080

Use this bulletin board to motivate students to work hard and study. When each student hands in work that is "tuned up," print his name on a car and add it to the bulletin board. Use the car pattern and make as many as you will need. The class goal would be to make as long a line of traffic as possible!

Use this bulletin board to encourage students to read more and discover the value of learning through reading. Duplicate the car pattern and write a reading activity on each for your students to complete. Things to read could include books, magazines, instructions, articles, newspapers, letters, maps, dictionaries, menus, signs, etc.

WE'RE TUNED UP FOR A GREAT YEAR

Use this bulletin board to encourage a variety of health habits. Have a class discussion about what things you should do each morning to keep you healthy—brushing teeth, washing your face, eating a nutritional breakfast. List each on an index card and add it to the bulletin board. Each morning that a student remembers to do all of these, let him add his name to the bulletin board.

53

GA1080

"CAR"-TOONS

Use this bulletin board to encourage students matching skills. Duplicate twelve or more car patterns in construction paper. Fold the comics into layers to save time and cut out the same amount of cars as you first did. Glue the comic car to the construction paper one to make it sturdier and then let dry. Cut each car in half and pin the pieces on the bulletin board. Challenge students to match up the correct pieces to make the "car"-toon go!

Use this bulletin board to display students' artwork. Discuss with your class things that are automated and let them design their own ideas. From automated swing sets to flying cars, encourage your designers to be inventive.

YOU "AUTO" LEARN THESE COLORS!

Use this bulletin board to teach students to recognize colors and identify them by name. Duplicate cars from the car pattern, making one of each color. Add the color's name and pin to the board. For some extra fun, play a game by asking students which cars match their clothing.

54

Use this bulletin board to teach students about good nutrition and the importance of having a balanced diet. Make a car for each student from the pattern, and every time he eats a healthy food, he can fill it up by writing in his healthy selection. Encourage each student to fill up his car and be in the driver's seat with good nutrition.

Student's Name

IS ROLLING ALONG IN _____

_____
Signed

GA1080

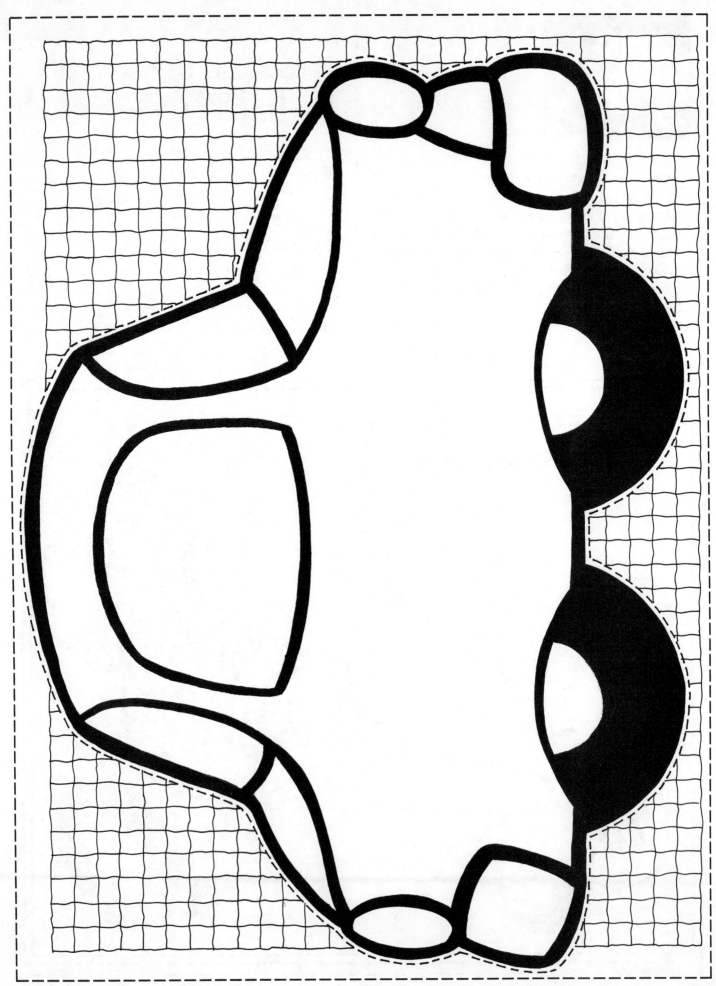

56

GA1080

RABBITS

57

GA1080

Theme for the Month: RABBITS

Keep your classroom hopping with the following unit. Students will love these furry friends as you inhabit your classroom with rabbits.

Use this Door Delighter to welcome students to your class. Make as many bunnies as you will need from the pattern below and write a student's name on each one. Add the bunnies to the door, and after taking them down, reuse them as name tags for a special event.

Use this bulletin board to strengthen students' math skills. Write the math problem on the ears and the corresponding answer on the face. Instruct students to match each pair of rabbit ears with the face that displays the correct answer. Ears and faces can be stored in envelopes attached to the board.

58

GA1080

Use this bulletin board as an assignment center to motivate students to carefully follow directions. Place a library card pocket on the bulletin board for each student with his name on it. Instruct each student to check his pocket each morning for his daily assignments and read and follow directions carefully.

WE'RE ALL EARS FOR FOLLOWING DIRECTIONS

SUE SAM BO BETH BETTY

CATHY CARL DICK DARLA FAITH

HAVE A HOPPY DAY!

Susan helped me with my math. Jill

John helped me when I dropped my books. Jared

Ali smiled and said hello to me. Susan

"SOME BUNNY" SPECIAL

Use this bulletin board to encourage students to be aware of and notice their feelings. Use this bulletin board as a place students can write how they feel. Later encourage writing on the bulletin board things that others did that made them feel happy.

Use this bulletin board to encourage your students' appreciation of community workers. While studying a variety of careers, each student could write a report or tell about someone he thinks is special and why. Photographs of the nominees could be added to the board if you desire.

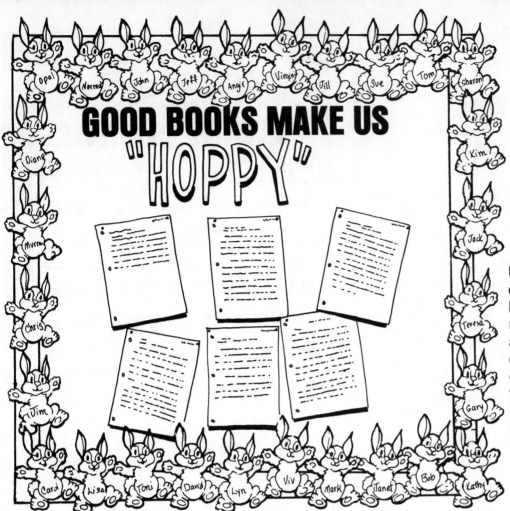

GOOD BOOKS MAKE US "HOPPY"

(rabbit border names: Opal, Norma, John, Jeff, Angie, Virginia, Jill, Sue, Tom, Sharon, Kim, Jack, Teresa, Gary, Diane, Murray, Chris, Jim, Carol, Lisa, Toni, David, Lyn, Viv, Mark, Janet, Bob, Kathy)

Use this bulletin board to display book jackets or book reports. Duplicate a rabbit for each student and add her name to it. If you desire, you could have students sign their rabbit each time they read one of the books displayed or of their own choosing.

Bunny Tales

Use this bulletin board to inspire a creative writing lesson. Discuss the difference between fiction and nonfiction and have your students write make-believe stories.

GA1080

LOOK WHO IS LISTENING

Use this bulletin board to encourage students to listen carefully. Whenever you catch a student using his listening skills, praise him by letting him add his name to the bulletin board.

Use this bulletin board to display school events. Put students in charge of keeping the board updated and feel free to include everything from school workers' birthdays to special holiday dates.

GA1080

Use this bulletin board to encourage students to work hard in math. Display work that students are proud of and rotate it weekly. This board could be used for a variety of subjects, so change the subject title as needed.

Student's Name

IS
"SOME BUNNY"
SPECIAL!

GA1080

GA1080

PLANET/GLOBE

GA1080

Theme for the Month: # PLANET/GLOBE

Use this bulletin board to motivate students to learn about the world around them. From sea to shining sea, here's a unit filled with facts from far away or right next door.

Use this Door Delighter to welcome students to your classroom world. Cut a circle for each student and let him color in his world and add his name. Show students actual pictures of the world and talk about all the different shapes which represent various places.

A WORLDLY WELCOME

KIM Don Jan

Lou Rick

DAVE

PAT Sam

Marta

Opal Mark

Tom

65

GA1080

OUR WORLD OF EVENTS

Duplicate the globe pattern for each student and use this bulletin board as a way to encourage students' awareness of current events. Place each student's globe on the bulletin board with his name on it and a specific country or location. Student must search for current events happening there and add them to his globe.

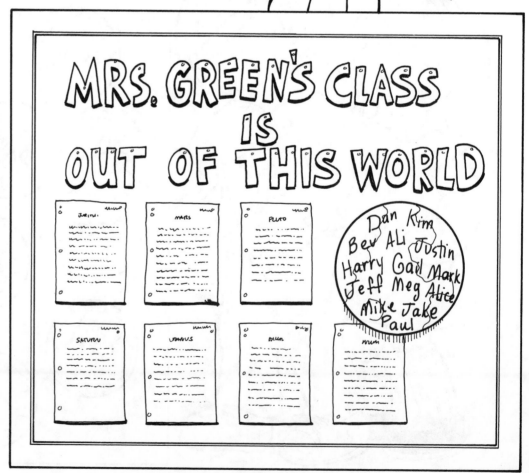

Use this bulletin board to welcome students to your classroom. Add each student's name to a globe and assign him a particular planet. Add students' reports about their planets to the bulletin board when completed. Younger students could illustrate the outer limits, and this board could be used to exhibit their artwork.

MRS. GREEN'S CLASS IS OUT OF THIS WORLD

66

Here's a bulletin board perfect for reinforcing math skills. Duplicate as many planets as you desire and write a math problem on each. Challenge students to soar their way through the problems and write their answers on paper.

Use this bulletin board to encourage learning about space and our solar system. To the stars on the board, add new facts each day which deal with space. Have students make fact finder lists and record the entries.

67

GA1080

Use this bulletin board to teach visual discrimination and pattern matching skills. Duplicate a pair of Saturn patterns for each student and have him color them in with patterns. Place one of each pair in an envelope on the board and staple the others in place. Challenge students to prevent the pattern from being lost in space by finding its matching mate.

Student's Name

IS
SOARING
WITH
SUPER WORK

GA1080

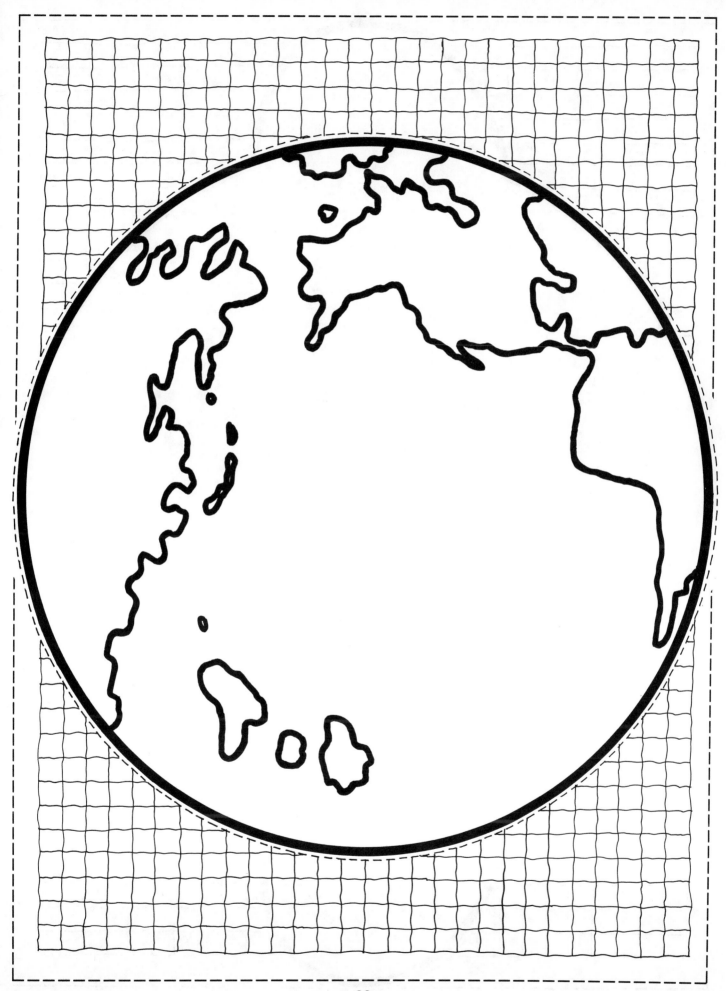

69

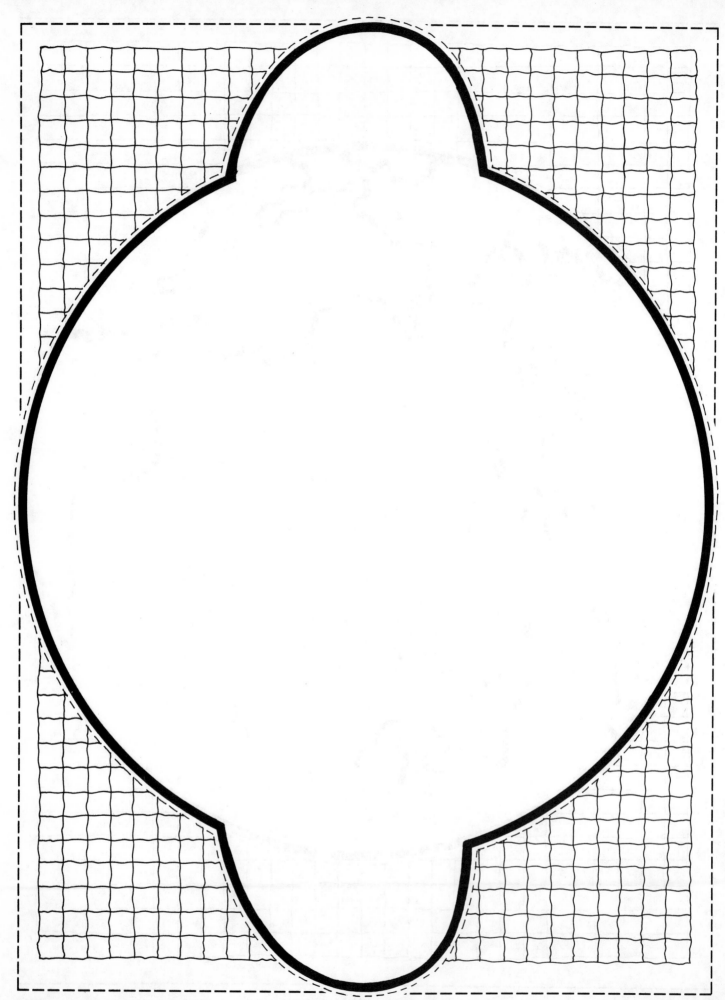

CAMERAS

71

Theme for the Month: CAMERAS

Here's a super Door Delighter to welcome students with their own friendly faces. Add students' photographs to the door and make sure they say "Cheese" as they enter each day.

PICTURE PERFECT

SPELLING SURE SHOTS

Use this bulletin board as a fun way to encourage students to learn to spell. Place pictures of objects that are on your students' spelling list on the bulletin board. By each picture place a vegetable carton from the grocery store. Have a class game where each student throws a piece of wadded paper at a picture. If he gets it in the carton, he scores a point. He earns five additional points if he can then spell correctly the name of the object.

72

GA1080

Use this bulletin board to encourage students to read more. Duplicate the camera pattern and list books from your reading list on each. Every time a student reads one of the books, let him sign his name on the bulletin board border.

ZOOM IN ON THESE BOOKS

Use this bulletin board to encourage a creative writing activity. Have students write descriptions and clues about something they picture on index cards. Add the cards to the board and see how many cards students can guess correctly.

73

GA1080

FOCUS YOUR ATTENTION ON THESE WORDS

STATE

COUNT

MONDAY

OFTEN

Use this bulletin board to encourage students to use complete sentences and to be able to speak before a group. Instruct each student to choose one of the words written on the cameras and use it to make a complete sentence. Have each student say his sentence out loud to the class.

Use this bulletin board to display student work that you are proud of. Let students choose their "hang-ups" to further encourage their sense of being neat and careful.

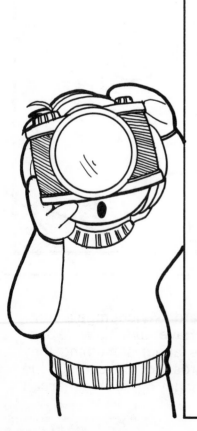

GOOD WORK WE'VE DEVELOPED

GA1080

A FINISH LINE PHOTO

Give each student a picture from a magazine and cut it in half. Have student glue half of the picture on a piece of paper and challenge him to finish the picture. Display these on the bulletin board.

Use this bulletin board to display student artwork. Encourage students to bring in photographs of themselves and their families. Talk about what makes each person different and discuss what features we have that make each of us unique. From freckles to the color of the eyes to the shape of the face, help students be aware of themselves and others. Next have students draw a self or family portrait and color them in with crayons or markers. Add each student's work to the board and create the bulletin board border with the photographs.

GA1080

WE'RE DEVELOPING GOOD MANNERS

Use this bulletin board to encourage good manners. Generate a class discussion and write students' ideas about manners on index cards. Add them to the bulletin board and praise your students as they exhibit them daily.

_____'S WORK
IS PICTURE PERFECT

GA1080

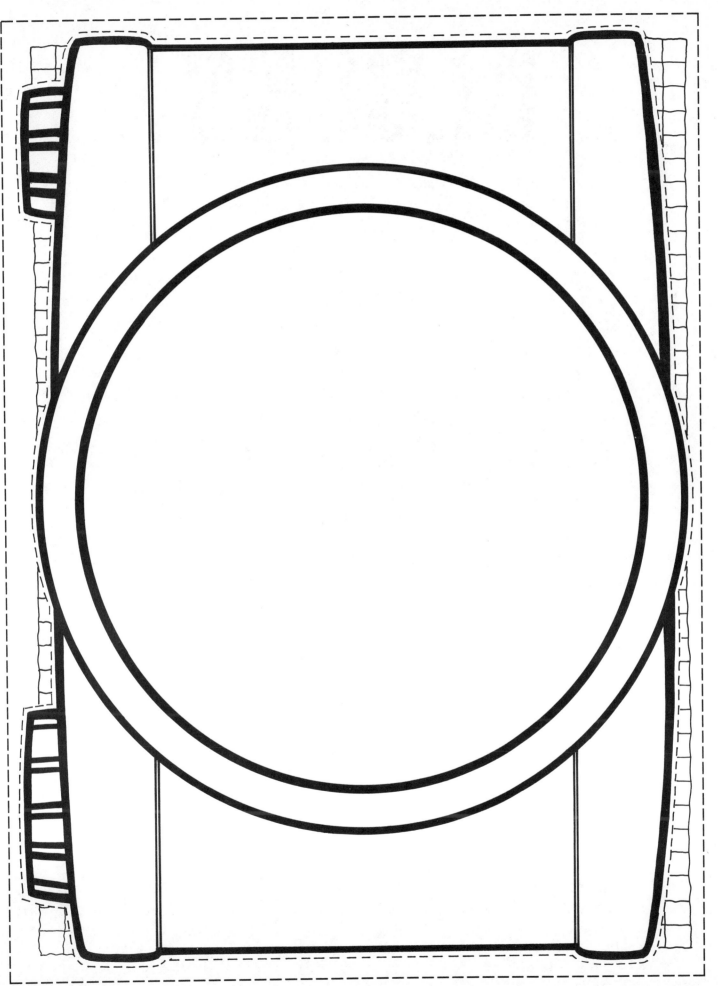

77

GA1080

CLOCKS

GA1080

Theme for the Month: # CLOCKS

Use this Door Delighter as an around-the-clock way to welcome students to your class. Duplicate a clock for each student and have him add his name and the time he was born to the clock. Fun additions include also bringing in baby pictures and guessing who's who.

Use this bulletin board to highlight students' reading record. Duplicate a clock for each student, make the hands from construction paper and add a metal brad to the center so the hands can move. Add student's name and place the clock on the bulletin board. Each time he reads a book from the reading list, move the hands of the clock forward an hour. The goal of the class should be to make it to midnight.

GA1080

Use this bulletin board to encourage good manners. Each time a student exhibits good manners, award him with a ticket. When a student earns ten tickets, let him purchase something from your class store. Include items in the store like a free-time pass for five minutes, crayons, a bookmark, recycled odds and ends, etc. Write the item on each clock, duplicated from the pattern. Students can also add their names to the board each time they earn purchases.

TAKE TIME FOR GOOD MANNERS

Sara — TIME PASS
PENCIL CASE
Eric — COLORED MARKER
Mark — Bookmark
DANNY — NOTE PAD
INK PEN
Leon
HEIDI

CLASS STORE

REDEEM TICKETS HERE

80

GA1080

Use this bulletin board to encourage students to use the dictionary. Discuss how the dictionary is important as a study tool and why it is helpful. Add three envelopes to the bulletin board. Create a variety of dictionary activities and place some in each. Examples: Find and list five words that have three syllables. Find and record ten words that have two syllables, or record the last word found under each letter of the alphabet.

Use this bulletin board to encourage students to be aware of their feelings. Have a class discussion about what makes each student feel good and duplicate a clock with his name on it. Instruct students to add what makes them tick to the clocks and display them on the bulletin board.

81

GA1080

Use this bulletin board as a fun way to encourage students to practice math skills. Duplicate clocks from the pattern and write a math problem on each. Have students "catch" time from running out by solving the problems correctly.

TIME'S RUNNING OUT

4+7

7+8

8-3

6+2

5+4

3+5

82

GA1080

Table Topper

Materials:

paper plates
construction paper
metal brads
crayons

1. Instruct students to cut out one long hand and one short hand from construction paper. Add the hands to the center of the clock by overlapping them at their base and piercing them with a metal brad. Attach to the center of the paper plate.
2. Add the numbers of the clock in order to the paper plate face.
3. Encourage each student to add a design of his choice with crayons and create a personality for his clock.
4. Clocks can be hung from the ceiling or stapled to another at the top so that they are back to back and will stand up on the table.

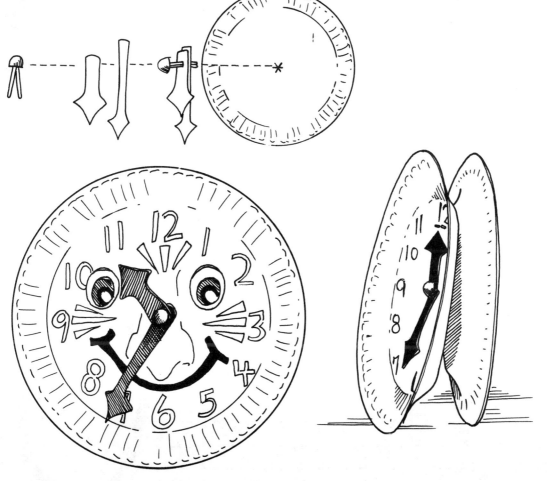

GA1080

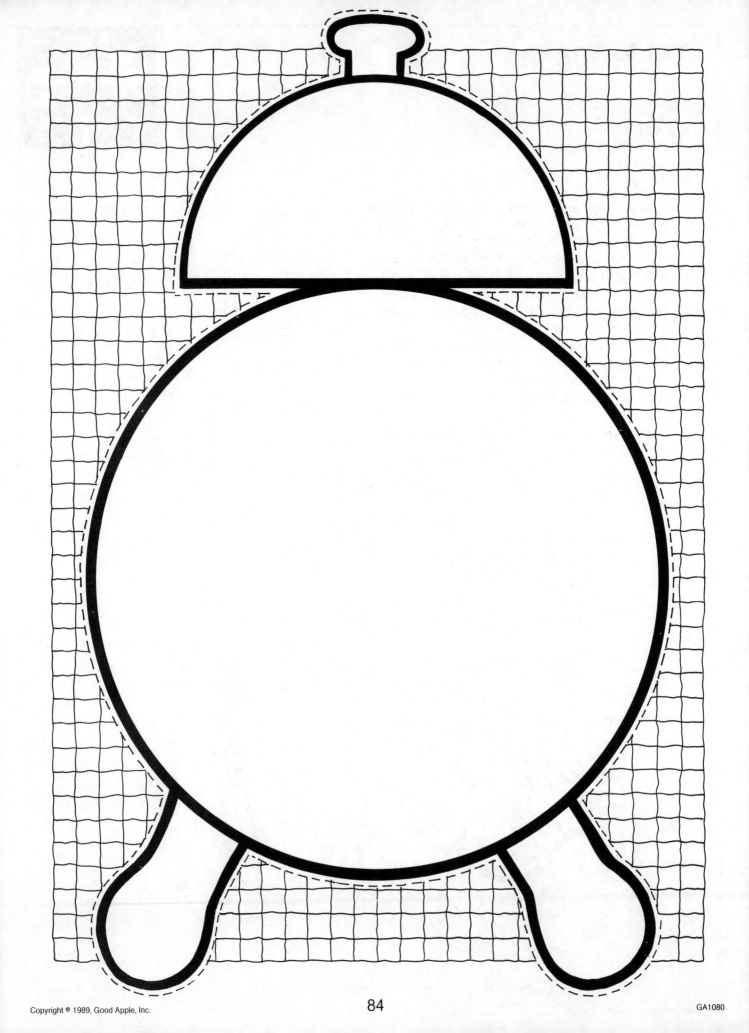

84

MAGICIAN

GA1080

Theme for the Month: MAGICIAN

Here's a month of magical units sure to cast their spell on your students.

Use this Door Delighter to welcome all who enter your classroom. Add each student's picture to the door and watch those smiles appear as they enter your classroom door.

OPEN SAYS ME!

Our Good Work's Appearing

Use this bulletin board to motivate students to do good work in a variety of subjects. Be specific and choose an area in which students may perform better. From neatness to following directions, this board will provide content for any improved skill.

GA1080

Use this bulletin board to summarize what students have learned in a subject. Instruct each student to write a report about the things he has learned and display on the bulletin board.

Use this bulletin board to encourage your students to hand in neat work. Each time a student does work that is neat, let him add his proof to the bulletin board.

SHOW STOPPERS

Use this bulletin board to motivate your students toward a goal you wish them to reach. Duplicate a top hat and rabbit for each student and write his name on it. Tuck a rabbit inside the hat so that it can be pulled out gradually. Each time the student makes progress, let him pull his rabbit out a little more until he's all the way out and he has stopped the show!

GA1080

DON'T LET APRIL FOOL YOU

Use this bulletin board as a graffiti board for students to write their jokes on. Let students read the jokes and try to answer them and if they can, they get to add one of their own.

ABRACADABRA

_____
Student's Name

SUPER WORK HAS APPEARED!

_____
Signed

88

89

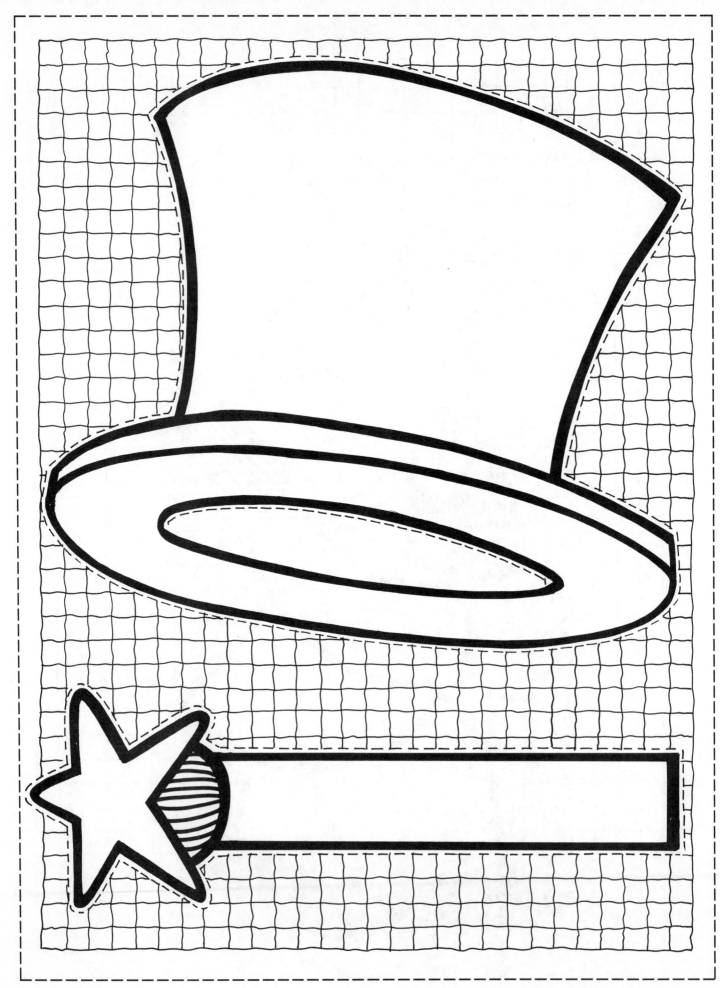

90

GA1080

MONEY

92

Theme for the Month: **MONEY**

Here's a unit sure to bring you a wealth of ideas. Your students will love cashing in on any of these.

Here's a Door Delighter sure to welcome your students. Duplicate a piggy bank for each student and add his name. Each time a student does something that allows you to count on him, from good manners to careful listening, he could add a paper penny or a sticker to his bank.

Use this bulletin board to encourage students learning specific facts. Duplicate a bank for each student and when he masters a particular subject or lesson, he gets to color in a coin in his bank.

93

GA1080

Use this bulletin board to teach students color and number recognition. Place a variety of objects that are different colors in an envelope and pin three pockets on the bulletin board. Instruct students to select an object and file it in its proper place. Pockets could be identified by color or descriptions of their amounts.

Use this bulletin board to encourage students to read the newspaper and reinforce a variety of reading skills. Refer to the money pattern and duplicate as many as you will need for each student. On each bill, write a task for students to search for while reading one page of the newspaper. Activities could include listing three-syllable words, listing verbs, listing pronouns, listing nouns, listing adverbs, etc.

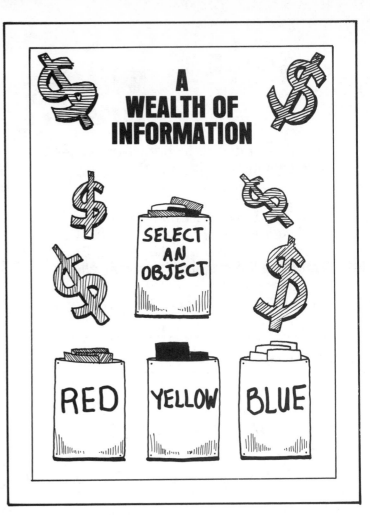

GA1080

Use this bulletin board to motivate students to study more. Add a bank to the board for each student, and when he studies, let him pin or staple a coin to his bank. Correct work can also be displayed on this board to really show that studying pays.

Use this bulletin board to encourage students to choose one New Year's resolution or weekly goal to strive for. Students' names can be put on paper plate pennies, and as they make changes towards their goals, use a hole punch to punch holes to acknowledge their progress.

Use this bulletin board to encourage students' interest in science. Display interesting work, book reports or facts on this bulletin board.

95

GA1080

Table Topper

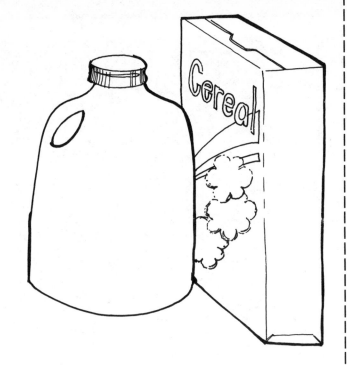

Materials:

empty clean bleach bottle, cereal box or container
scrap construction paper
odds and ends
scissors
glue

To Begin:

1. Encourage students to make their own table toppers by creating banks.
2. Assist students, if necessary, with the basic slit for the money and help them cut the containers if needed.
3. Students can transform their containers into characters, spaceships or objects of their choice by adding paper scraps and odds and ends to top it off.

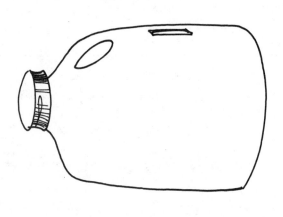

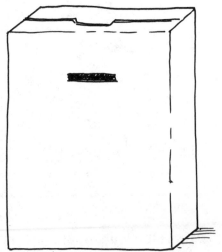

GA1080

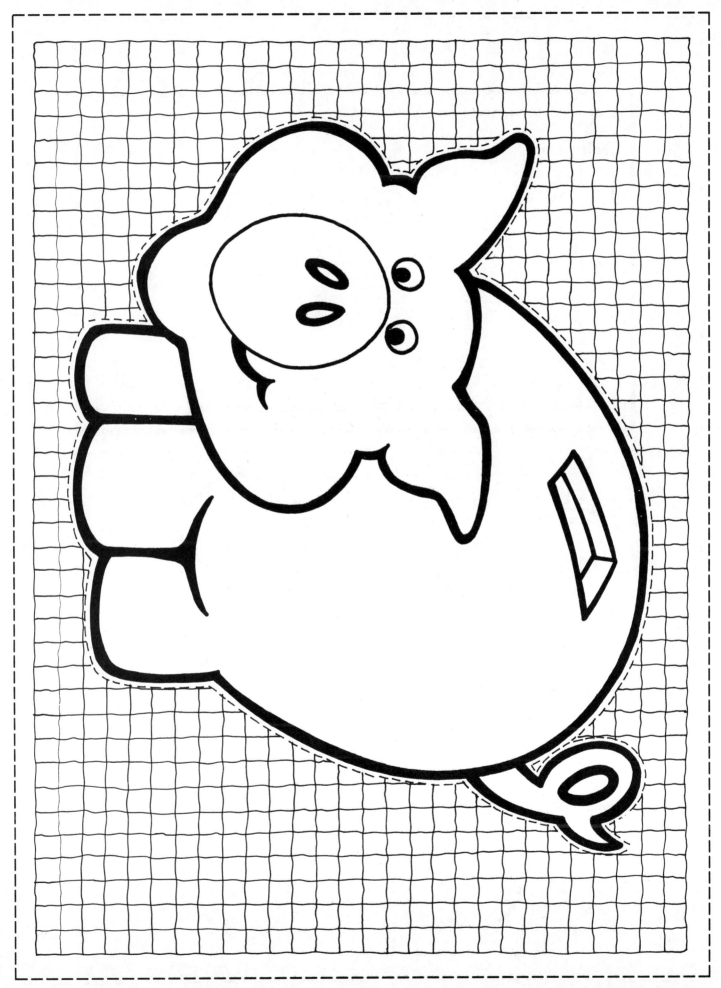

97

GA1080

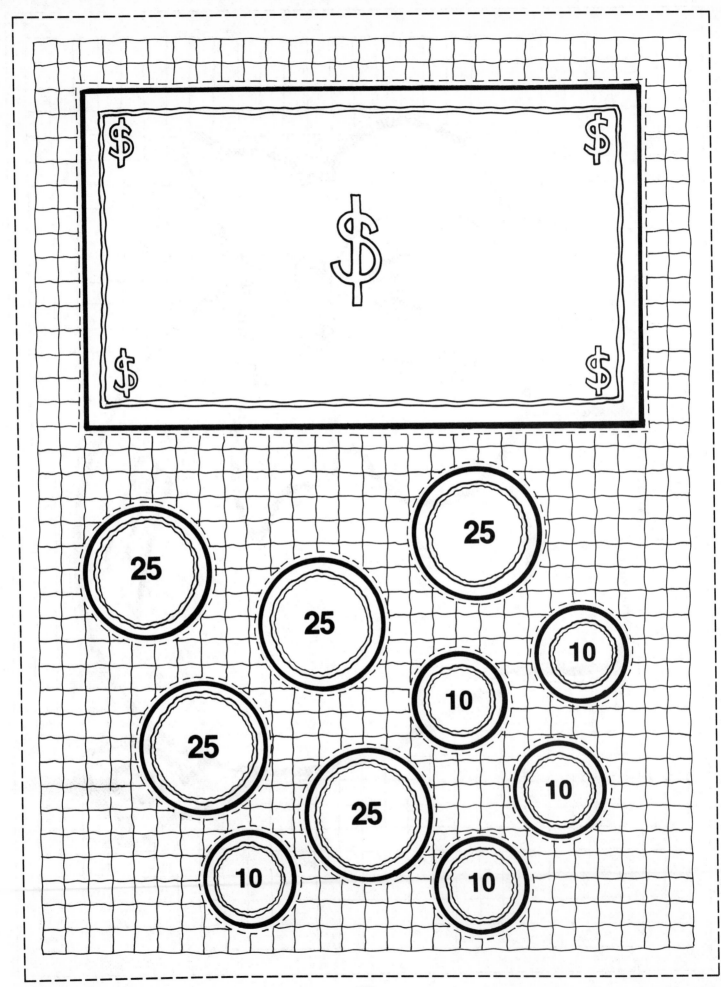

GA1080

DRAGONS

99

GA1080

Theme for the Month: DRAGONS

Here's a unit filled with ideas hot off the press. Your students will really get fired up with a theme that won't leave them "dragon"!

Use this Door Delighter to welcome students to your class. Students' names can be written on index cards and later be used as name cards for a special event.

MR. SMITH'S HOT SHOTS

CARLA
Tyler
Mark
Helen
Dione
Clark
JAN
Maggie
Tina
Kirk
John

MRS. MAY'S CLASS IS FIRED UP

Terry
CLARK
DON
TiNA
Jill
Shanon
Virginia
Brandon
Alen
Casey
Bob

Use this bulletin board to introduce your students in your class. Students' names can be added to the bulletin board.

GA1080

Use this bulletin board to motivate good nutrition in your students. Discuss the four basic food groups and encourage student involvement in menu planning. Whenever a student eats a balanced meal, let him trace his handprint on the bulletin board or cut it out from paper and pin it in place.

GOOD NUTRITION WON'T LEAVE YOU "DRAGON"

Use this bulletin board to display facts in any subject area which you want your students to learn.

WORK WE'RE FIRED UP ABOUT

Use this bulletin board to exhibit student work. Instruct students to hand in their home-work on time, and when they do, let each one put up a "hang-up" he is especially proud of.

GA1080

Use this bulletin board to motivate students in a creative writing exercise. Have students write stories about something that was too hot to handle and what happened. Here's a perfect opportunity to learn about who, what, when and why. Students can underline each of the four answers in their stories.

Use this bulletin board to teach students about categories and to use the library for research. Refer to the dragon pattern and duplicate four of them, one for each envelope. Label each with a season—winter, spring, summer and fall. Instruct students to keep a record of subjects which belong in each category. The goal for each student would be to make as long a list as he can in the determined time period.

GA1080

Use this bulletin board to encourage students to increase their vocabularies. Reuse the dragon and let him go to work popping popcorn. Duplicate the popcorn pattern for each student and add his name. Add popcorn shapes to the board, and each time a student learns an additional vocabulary word he gets to add it to his piece.

Use this bulletin board to inspire a creative writing lesson. Have each student write an opening sentence to an imaginative story and then trade sentences. Students can challenge each other to use the sentences as starters to their dragon "tales."

GA1080

WHICH KNIGHT IS RIGHT?

$$\begin{array}{c}4\\+7\\\hline 12\end{array}\qquad\begin{array}{c}3\\+8\\\hline 11\end{array}\qquad\begin{array}{c}2\\+4\\\hline 5\end{array}\qquad\begin{array}{c}1\\+7\\\hline 8\end{array}$$

$$\begin{array}{c}2\\+6\\\hline 8\\+3\\\hline 9\end{array}\qquad\begin{array}{c}3\\-1\\\hline 1\\+6\\\hline 7\end{array}$$

Use this bulletin board to strengthen students' math skills. Add a knight in shining armour to the dragon on the bulletin board and display a variety of addition or subtraction problems on index cards. Add some right answers and include some that are incorrect. Challenge students to a duel and let them record which problems are right. Students will love taking turns at changing the problems daily as they try to fool their classmates.

Student's Name

IS FIRED UP IN

Signed

104

GA1080

105